READY, SET, COOK

HOW TO MAKE GOOD FOOD WITH WHAT'S ON HAND

(no fancy skills, fancy equipment, or fancy budget required)

DAWN PERRY

SIMON & SCHUSTER

New York   London   Toronto   Sydney   New Delhi

Simon & Schuster
1230 Avenue of the Americas
New York, NY 10020

First Simon & Schuster hardcover edition November 2021

SIMON & SCHUSTER and colophon are registered trademarks of Simon & Schuster, Inc.

For information about special discounts for bulk purchases,
please contact Simon & Schuster Special Sales at
1-866-506-1949 or business@simonandschuster.com.

The Simon & Schuster Speakers Bureau can bring authors to your live event. For
more information or to book an event, contact the Simon & Schuster Speakers Bureau
at 1-866-248-3049 or visit our website at www.simonspeakers.com.

Designed by George McCalman and Aliena Cameron of McCalmanCo.

Manufactured in China

1   3   5   7   9   10   8   6   4   2

Library of Congress Cataloging-in-Publication Data has been applied for.

ISBN 978-1-9821-4726-6
ISBN 978-1-9821-4727-3 (ebook)

At the beginning of quarantine, which coincided with the bulk of my recipe development for this book, I wrote down and often posted publicly a daily gratitude list. Many days the list included things like butter, salt, and terrible streaming reality TV shows. What it didn't always include were the names of the individuals who made the writing of this book (and my day-to-day life) pretty easy, all things considered.

My deepest gratitude to my mom and dad, my sisters and their families for their unconditional love and endless good humor. I would choose you even if I wasn't lucky enough to call you family. To the Duckors for their love, support, and interest in the process.

Thank you to my agent, Kristin van Ogtrop: for your wit, smarts, and willingness to stick with me as I kneaded a half-baked idea into something worth sharing. I am so grateful for your guidance, your belief in me, and for that one time you told me I might be the most likeable person in New York City.

Thank you to the friends, family, and gifted cooks who tested the recipes in this book, for lending their time and skills: Theo Kaloudis, Mardi Miskit, Sanaë Lemoine, Charlyne Mattox, Sara Tane, Ananda Eidelstein, Grace Elkus, Greg Brownstein, Danielle Walsh, Eliza Lucas, Sarah Manganiello, Mollie Chen, and Rob Bonstein.

Thank you to my food friends, former colleagues, teachers, and students for helping me see food and cooking through so many different lenses. My deepest thanks to Adeena Sussman, Angela Cha, Antoni Porowski, Ben Mims, Claire Saffitz, Ethan Frisch, Grace Hahn, Jenny Rosenstrach, Jing Gao, Lior Lev Sercarz, Nik Sharma, and Sue Li for your kind words and helpful insights.

Thank you to Pam Zola, Kelly Keyes, Kari Woldum, Lauren Perth, Leah Pearson, Nancy Feig, Nancy Cha, Kate Ball, Tracy Wasserman, Erin Berlant Haggerty, the Bocar-Passettes, and the Wilsons for years of friendship and feedback and for never needing a backstory.

Thank you to the best shoot crew in the biz for your focus, laughter, free dance, and deep breaths. To photographer David Malosh for being honest, forgiving, and a consummate host; to prop stylists Megan Hedgepeth and John Lingenfelter, for making laid-back look really lovely. And to Jess Damuck: It never feels like work with you.

Thank you to the artists who helped make the proposal and finished product look so damn fine. To Alyce Jones for communicating in the proposal's design what I didn't always have the language for. Thank you to Ali Cameron for your easy laugh, great glasses, and impeccable email response time. Thank you to designer and guru George McCalman for your decades of friendship and camaraderie, for knowing me so well and seeing me so fully, and for illustrating all of that in these pages.

To my brilliant editor Emily Graff: Thank you for your patience and enthusiasm throughout this process. The day we met I was sweaty, pregnant, and very scattered. Thank you for putting me at ease that day and every Friday since. Thank you to Brittany Adames and Lashanda Anakwah, to Jackie Seow, Ruth Mui-Lee, Beth Maglione, Samantha Hoback, Elizabeth Herman, Alyssa diPierro, Kimberly Goldstein, Rafael Taveras, Maxwell Smith and the rest of the team at Simon & Schuster for your time, input, and expertise.

Thank you, Matt, my cheerleader and champion. And to Ramona, and Russell, for keeping everything in perspective. It's all for you.

With love,
DP

INTRODUCTION

PART 1
WHAT TO BUY

PART 2
WHAT TO MAKE

PART 3
WHAT TO COOK

LET'S ROLL!

INTRO DUCTION

LET'S TALK ABOUT THE PANTRY

I didn't plan dinner tonight. But I'm not stressed. I pulled some salmon out of the freezer at lunchtime. I have some boiled potatoes in the fridge, and I'll toss some green beans with a little vinaigrette. Dinner will be ready in no time.

I didn't always cook this way. About fifteen years ago, I was hanging out with some friends after a celebratory evening on the town. We came home to their Brooklyn apartment and we needed a snack, stat. Too hungry to wait for pizza delivery, I started digging through the fridge and cupboard. I can't remember if they challenged me or if I took it on myself, but I was determined to make something delicious out of whatever they had on hand.

I was twenty-six, just getting my start in editorial food—that's industryspeak for writing recipes for magazines—and was still hung up on the "nose to tail, root to tip, know your farmer by their first name" food snobbery that plagues a lot of young food professionals. These are all good things—certainly better for the planet—but swing too far in that righteous direction, and these views can be narrow at best and condescending at worst. Organic and ethically sourced ingredients are a priority for me, but there have been times in my life when the best I could afford was conventional produce and supermarket-brand staples. I'm not going to tell someone they can't or shouldn't cook for themselves and their family because something's too expensive or too hard to find.

But back to that night in Brooklyn. Perhaps it was necessity that softened my snobbery (or the alcohol). There were no market-fresh vegetables in the crisper, no aged cheddar in the deli drawer. I found a couple handfuls of pregrated cheese, half a box of penne, a little milk (skim, I think), and a bag of flour. I got it!

Cut to the three of us perched on the edge of the plush gray sofa, hands cupping steaming bowls of stovetop mac and cheese, friends impressed, all of us satisfied. An idea started to twinkle. What if cooking could be this fun and fast and easy all the time? No long grocery lists, no special market trips, but accessible, convenient, and at my fingertips.

I am a cook by trade. I got my start after college when, at a friend's suggestion, I moved to the Bay Area (Jen: "I'm moving to San Francisco and I think you should come with me." Me: "OK!"). I was bright-eyed, bushy-tailed, and without direction. So I did what any practical person would do: I went to culinary school. Soon I found a job as a prep cook in a restaurant. Every grain of farro, every foraged mushroom, every fairy tale eggplant was from within a hundred miles of our kitchen and always peak-season perfect. Fish caught just that morning arrived on ice at the back door. Sides of beef and whole lambs came from nearby farms with noble-sounding names, like Kicking Bull and Don Watson. I once transported a whole hog, on the back seat of my car, from "Chez"—as they called Chez Panisse, in Berkeley—back to the city for that week's dinner service (I put down a tarp).

> What if cooking could be fun and fast and easy all the time?

Every day was a market day: Tuesdays I was in the East Bay, Thursdays and Sundays I drove to Marin County. Nothing rivals the bounty of the Ferry Plaza Farmers Market at San Francisco's Embarcadero on a Saturday. One time I drove ninety minutes to pick fresh laurel leaves from some guy's yard. We drank plum wine under a tree in the garden. It was a very nice afternoon.

Hunting and gathering ingredients, no matter how or from how far, was just part of the night's dinner prep, and as important as the cooking itself. I loved it.

I held tight to these beliefs for a long time, while I cooked in restaurants and as a private chef, and even after I moved to New York and started working in test kitchens. I spent my time at work writing recipes for home cooks using special ingredients and complicated techniques (seaweed and tofu beignets, croquembouche, a three-day pork terrine en croûte). Cooking those fancy recipes was fun, but I didn't often make them again when I got home. After a long day, I was too tired to stop at three different markets to pick up wakame, chicken livers, or two more dozen eggs.

And then, on that night fifteen years ago in Brooklyn, I was reminded of how much good food you can make with what's on hand. Many smart home cooks know this already, especially working parents. But for young, ambitious me, it was a real forehead-slapping moment. I knew this implicitly, but had been so focused on trying to impress folks with fancy techniques and ingredients that I was missing the good stuff right under my nose. That was not what I had been taught as a novice restaurant cook.

That's what inspired the many recipes I wrote at *Bon Appétit* and later *Real Simple*, where I led our test kitchen as food director. I wanted good food, fast, that was beautiful to look at and delicious

to eat but didn't take more than a half hour of hands-on time. I wanted to make cooking easy and approachable by writing recipes that called for what you already had on hand. I used the tricks I had picked up in my training along the way, from restaurant chefs and home cooks and my family, too, makers of my favorite salad dressing (more on that later). But now, instead of hunting and gathering ingredients, I got more satisfaction out of using the items I kept in my own pantry.

I used to think of this as laziness. But I have two little kids now. I'm married, over forty (how?). I'm less interested in spending my mornings and weekends sourcing, schlepping, and prepping ingredients for an eight-hour Bolognese than I am in just sitting down for a minute. My guess is you have other stuff you'd like to be doing with your free time and energy, too. If so, it's time to stock your pantry.

"Pantry" isn't just a name for a cupboard with shelves, and it doesn't mean dry goods alone. Your pantry is made up of all the long-lasting ingredients you use on a regular basis, whether they live in the cupboard, the fridge, or the freezer. My pantry is a combination of versatile ingredients I can find at any supermarket plus a collection of homemade staples—what will transform a bowl of plain pasta to nutty, creamy, cheesy bliss.

If you're worried you picked up a meal-planning manifesto, that's not what this is. This book will teach you how to make meals with what you have on hand (eggs, potatoes, vinegar), not what you wish you could find (flowering broccoli) or wish you had started three weeks ago (preserved lemons). Whether you're new to cooking and want to know where to start, or you're a pro and need to streamline your approach (new kids, new outlook, new work-from-home routine), this book will get you ready and set you up for success so you can cook quickly,

> Your pantry is made up of all the long-lasting ingredients you use on a regular basis, whether they live in the cupboard, the fridge, or the freezer.

easily, and flexibly at a moment's notice. No fancy skills, fancy equipment, or fancy budget required.

The first step is stocking your pantry. In part 1, I list my favorite easy-to-find pantry ingredients. These are the ones I can't cook without. I've lived and cooked in big cities and small towns all over the country, and I can say with confidence that you can find almost all of these ingredients at your local supermarket or corner grocery. You probably have a lot of these ingredients in your pantry already.

Depending on where you grew up, your cultural background, travels, and personal preferences, your pantry will look a little (or a lot) different from mine. It's what I love about cooking and learning alongside other home cooks. I can't wait to hear how you incorporate your favorite pantry ingredients into some of these recipes. (They're flexible like that.) Whatever you have on hand, whatever you love, use it.

In part 2, I explain how to build on your existing cache of store-bought ingredients by making and stocking a handful of homemade staples. I call them *Pantry+ Ingredients*. Nothing crazy: a vinaigrette from the olive oil and vinegar you have on hand, or an easy marinara from a can of tomatoes, for example. I don't expect you to have every one of these Pantry+ Ingredients all of the time, but having just a few at the ready can add flavor, texture, and interest to your meals.

In part 3, we put it all together. Versatile store-bought ingredients and homemade staples add up to delicious, fast, and flexible meals you can make any time of day, any day of the week without a ton of

effort, time, or money. You'll find recipes for quick and healthy breakfasts, easy dinners, and veggies and sides to round things out. There are snacks to nosh on and sweets to indulge in, because we should all live a little. Or a lot.

During the 180 months since the global pandemic hit (What's that? It's only been 18? . . . Oh.) we've all been cooking a lot more at home. For some, it's the first time they've prepared three meals a day. Others have swung from overseeing cold cereal prep and packing school lunches to running a full-service, fast-casual restaurant out of their home kitchen. With no prep cook. Even if you were an avid home cook before, the contents and cadence of your cooking have changed. I've come to rely on my pantry more than ever; maybe you have, too.

Pantry cooking isn't just a hook for this book—it's how I cook in real life. It's how all talented home cooks get food on the table day in and day out. Thinking about and touching food all day can zap an appetite (and motivation) by the time dinner rolls around. Having a flexible, easy-to-use pantry at the ready keeps tired professional cooks from eating cereal and peanut butter straight out of the jar for every meal. More than that, it helps you cook with greater economy and less waste. When you know what's on hand and how to use it, you're less likely to spend money on ingredients you already have or won't use up before they go bad. And we should all strive for that.

This book is a snapshot of my pantry: the ingredients I love, the things I use often. I hope it inspires you to build, maintain, and use yours.

Are you ready? Get set. Let's cook.

A WELL-STOCKED PANTRY MEANS A GOOD MEAL IS ONLY MINUTES AWAY.

PART I

WHAT TO BUY

Stocking your pantry can feel like a big investment at first, especially if you're starting from scratch. Buy the best ingredients you have access to. In the long run, a pantry filled with high-quality, practical groceries helps you make *good* meals *fast*.

WHERE TO START

Before you invest, take a hard look at your existing pantry. If you're starting from scratch, you're in luck. It's way easier to outfit an empty kitchen than it is to evaluate all of your edible possessions with a neutral heart. (One friend remarked that going through her freezer was like looking at old vacation photos: "Aw, that's the bacon we picked up on that great trip to the Berkshires.")

Curating your pantry is a little like going through your clothes closet: if you haven't used an ingredient in the last six months, get rid of it. You're either not interested in it or it could use replacing.

While you're at it, check the expiration date on everything. Remember, your pantry includes your cupboard, fridge, and freezer.

Look in your **cupboards**. Most dry goods last a really long time, but you'd be surprised how many items you've let sit around for more than two years after using them once. I once held on to a box of nonfat dried milk powder through two apartment moves. I used it to make white bread once; turns out I was not going to make it again anytime soon.

Now **check the fridge**. And not just the shelves. Go through the doors—where the biggest offenders, like too-hot hot sauce or weirdly textured jam can hide behind the ketchup—and get rid of any condiments you don't use monthly. Check crisper and deli drawers and throw away (or, bless you righteous ones, compost) the wilted, the faded, the moldy. While you're in there, go ahead and give surfaces a swipe with a damp sponge or disinfectant wipe. It's as satisfying as Swiffering the closet floor.

Finally, **look in the freezer**. Anything that's been in the deep freeze longer than three months should probably go. Some very new and well-calibrated freezers can keep things free of freezer burn for up to six months, but I've only encountered one of these appliances in my life. (For the record, this was an ex-boyfriend's mom's nothing-special freezer. One Christmas we ate lemon scones that had been frozen since the *previous* Christmas, reheated in the toaster oven. I chalk this up to her impeccable storage skills—individually double plastic wrapped, then sealed in a zippered plastic bag—but also to the fact that she never let the freezer get packed to the gills, limiting airflow, which is what can cause a big freeze.) Check inside bags and foil to identify anything mysterious: if it's covered in ice crystals, it will taste more like freezer than whatever it once was. Go ahead and get rid of it. You probably know this, but I recommend that you label stuff with a Sharpie before it goes into the freezer. No need for prose, just write what it is and when you put it in there.

Once you've given your pantry a good, honest evaluation, you'll start to see what ingredients you actually use. Favorite pieces—canned tomatoes, maybe, or even farro—will make themselves known just like a favorite pair of jeans.

WHAT TO
STOCK

You don't need to have every single one of these items on hand all the time, but if you have even some available *most* of the time, you can make dozens of meals even when it seems like there's nothing to eat in the house.

Consider this list a blueprint. If you're eager to stretch and try new flavors, know that your pantry will grow and change the more you cook from it. Start with some basics, and build from there.

The more you cook from your pantry, the more you'll start to notice ingredients you have that you actually love and use. Focus on those. Donate the rest if possible, or make a meal for a friend who loves sardines (or what have you).

THE CUPBOARD

While your pantry will soon consist of far more than dry ingredients, the bulk of your arsenal will still live in the cupboard. Why? Because dry and shelf-stable ingredients last a really, really long time. The only difference between your pantry and those end-of-days folks is that you won't buy more than can comfortably fit in your cabinet. No bunker necessary.

The items below are listed from, in my opinion, more essential to less so. The more you cook, the more you'll figure out what's absolutely necessary for you.

OILS

Olive oil is my go-to fat for most cooking. You've heard the news: it's good for you! Full of antioxidants, healthy monounsaturated fats, and anti-inflammatory properties, olive oil is indispensable for roasting or sautéing vegetables, searing chicken parts, building salad dressings, and drizzling over finished dishes like soup or pasta or simply steamed fish. California Olive Ranch makes a terrific-tasting and affordable oil that's available at most major supermarkets. Heat and light can destroy an oil's flavor, so choose dark bottles and keep them stored in a cool, dark place away from the stove.

You'll want a **neutral oil**, too. Safflower, grapeseed, and canola oils are all good choices. I use them interchangeably for high-heat cooking like stir-fries, cutlet frying, or searing steaks in a ripping-hot cast-iron pan. Compared to most olive oils, neutral-flavored oils have a high smoke point, that is, they can get really hot before turning to smoke, getting stinky, and making your food taste gross. Because they don't have a ton of flavor on their own, they're ideal for infusing with other flavors like the Quick Chili Oil on page 70. Store in a cool, dark place alongside your olive oil.

VINEGARS

I keep red wine, white wine, sherry, apple cider, balsamic, and rice wine vinegars on hand most of the time. I know that seems like a lot, but each vinegar has its own particular flavor. If you want to streamline your pantry, pick white wine vinegar. It's a great all-purpose vinegar you can use for brightening and balancing dressings and sauces as well as finished dishes. I'll call for other vinegars throughout the book, but know that you can always substitute your old standby, white wine vinegar.

KOSHER SALT

This is my all-purpose seasoning for cooking *and* baking. Warning: all kosher salts are not created equal. Look for Diamond Kosher salt (in a red and white box). It's the least salty of the salts (Morton's kosher salt is about one and a half times as salty as Diamond brand, while table salt is twice as salty). Kosher salt, because it's additive free, will last indefinitely.

> Vinegars vary wildly in quality. Don't be afraid to buy a few bottles of the same type. Even less desirable vinegars aren't yucky (so they won't go to waste), but, when tasted side by side, it'll be obvious to your tongue which you prefer.

BLACK PEPPERCORNS

Commit to buying whole Tellicherry peppercorns and a pepper grinder. Freshly ground pepper adds warmth and balance to savory dishes and even some baked goods (think dark chocolate ganache or cooked blackberries). I rarely measure pepper. If a recipe *does* call for a measured amount (Salt and Pepper Honey Nuts, page 283), know that twenty turns from most grinders equals about a quarter teaspoon of ground black pepper. Buy whole peppercorns and they'll last longer than it will take you to use them up.

RICE & GRAINS

Rice makes an inexpensive, versatile, and flavorful base, side, or even the star of a recipe. Browse the rice section of your supermarket and you'll see there are a *lot* of types to try, but I always have basmati or long grain brown rice around. Whichever type you pick, it should last several months in the pantry.

Regarding other grains, I keep **quinoa** and **farro** on hand all the time, too, because 1) I like them, 2) they're both pretty quick cooking, and 3) they have distinct flavors and textures but can stunt double for rice in most roles. Couscous is another good ingredient to keep around. It's technically a pasta, but it acts like a grain and cooks in five minutes, so two thumbs up.

PASTA & NOODLES

Even the slowest cooking pasta will be tender in fifteen minutes, making it my favorite fast-track meal option. Pick your favorite pasta shapes (spaghetti for me—I like to twirl) and never be without them. There's a lot written (and debated) about pairing the right noodle with the right sauce. And while, yes, there's a semolina grain of truth to some of those arguments—short tubes catch meaty ragus, wide noodles for creamy sauces to cling to—I say use what you've got. Except for baked pastas—tubes and other shorties are best for baking. They cook slower than skinny spaghetti and the like, making them more mush-averse and easier to scoop and serve. I also keep a package of buckwheat soba or curly ramen noodles on hand for Asian-inspired soups or tossing with veggies and a cold pantry sauce for a quick lunch.

ONIONS & GARLIC

I would rather my house smell like sautéed onions and garlic than anything the Yankee Candle company can bottle. Cooked hot and fast to deeply charred, or low and slow until melting and caramel colored, onions are the foundation of hundreds, thousands, maybe even *millions* of dishes the world over, from curries and chutneys to caramelized onion dip. I really can't cook without them. As far as alliums (that's an onion-type thing) go, I always have yellow and red onions on hand, probably a few shallots, and usually some scallions. And always garlic. Garlic adds heat and assertive flavor when added raw—I like to grate it on a Microplane—but mellows when cooked. Treat garlic with care. If you burn it, you're kind of stuck—it gets distractingly bitter and can ruin a whole pot of soup or sauce. If that happens, start over. And know that I've been there, too.

FLOUR & CORNMEAL

All-purpose flour (or an alternative gluten-free blend) is the foundation of most baked goods, and it does important work thickening gravy and stews, creating a nonstick work surface for rolling out dough, and more. All-purpose flour is by far the most versatile, but whole-grain flours like spelt, rye, or nut meals add wonderful complex flavor and can be easily incorporated into most recipes that call for all-purpose flour. Feel free to substitute up to a third of the amount of flour called for with one of these alternatives. I keep a bag of cornmeal around as well to add a bit of crunch and texture to baked goods (the same one-third rule applies) or fried things like the Scallion Corn Cakes on page 131.

TOMATOES

I'm never without a few types of canned and/or tubed tomatoes. I stock twenty-eight-ounce cans of whole peeled and crushed tomatoes, a tube or two of double concentrated tomato paste, and a jar of my favorite sauce (I'm particularly fond of Rao's marinara). Adjust the seasonings and tomatoes will open up your cooking to a world of flavors. Blend them into salsas (see page 82), simmer in a 15-Minute Marinara (see page 90), and add to curries, braises, and more.

BEANS

Canned chickpeas have long been my favorite legume. You'll find a handful of recipes—a roasted salmon, a simple curry, a fried rice—that lead with them, but feel free to use whatever canned beans are your favorite. I usually have two cans of chickpeas around, plus at least one can of black, pinto, cannellini, or kidney beans. I'm fond of cans with a pop top so I don't need a can opener (which I can never seem to find). Dried beans are a wonderful and economical staple, too, though they take a little more time and forethought before you can actually eat them. I've included a straightforward recipe (Adaptable Beans, page 104) that uses a pound of dried beans. Once cooked, a pound of beans will yield the same amount as four fifteen-ounce cans. Use them whenever canned beans are called for in recipes.

POTATOES & SWEET POTATOES

My preferred spuds are tiny gold potatoes and sweet potatoes. I boil or roast the little ones (I've listed a bunch of ways to use them on page 192). I slice and roast a few sweet potatoes with wedges of red onion almost every week—for an easy side, quick lunch addition, kid-friendly veg—and I try to remember to toss a whole sweet potato into the oven whenever I know it will be on for about an hour at 350-ish degrees, say, when I'm roasting a chicken or something. Stick them in the fridge until you're ready to use, then peel and add them to grits or polenta, or simply split while still warm, top with unsalted butter, and sprinkle with flaky salt.

DRIED SPICES

Your spice cabinet, like the rest of your pantry, will reflect your particular preferences, your cultural background, your interests, maybe even your travels. My favorite spices, the ones that make the most frequent appearance in this book, are ones that remind me of home (dried oregano, cinnamon, Old Bay) and those I've come to know and love after cooking with people from all over the world: cumin and coriander, fennel seed,

turmeric, bay leaves, and crushed red pepper flakes. This is my core collection. Used alone or alongside one another, they can be combined in dozens of ways. Later in this book (see page 52), I list some combinations for a few different flavor profiles, if you're looking for a place to start.

NUT (OR SEED) BUTTER

Few things please me like a peanut butter and jelly sandwich. That quintessential combination is reason enough to keep a jar of your favorite nutty spread in stock—try it on crackers or swirled into yogurt, and don't miss the Half-Baked Peanut Butter Pie (see page 302).

Tahini, too, is a must for me. This thick paste made from ground sesame seeds enriches dishes and adds nutty depth and a touch of bitterness to dressings, dips, sauces, and smoothies. You can even use it in place of mayo in egg or tuna salad. Cookbook author and tahini expert (she literally wrote a book on it!) Adeena Sussman suggests looking for tahini made with Ethiopian sesame seeds from the town of Humera where the most prized seeds are grown. She says that when you're in the store and pick up a jar, "you want to hear a slapping sound, like a can of paint, which indicates the tahini is still emulsified. If you hear more of a splash, it's likely separated, meaning that the jar's been on the shelf for a while." Adeena recommends Soom brand tahini, but Al Arz and Har Bracha are other reliable options.

OATS

Even if you're not a morning oatmeal person, oats have a place in your pantry. Use them as a gluten-free binder in

meatballs or to make homemade granola. Fold them into cookie dough for added texture and good-for-you fiber. If you have a high-powered blender you can even grind them up into oat flour (it's gluten-free!).

SUGAR, GRANULATED & BROWN

I keep granulated white sugar around for cookies, cakes, and other sweet stuff, but a pinch can also help to balance super tangy dressings or tomato sauce. It lasts forever. While dark brown sugar is slightly more sticky and flavorful than light brown sugar (because it contains more molasses left over from the refining process), feel free to use them interchangeably here. Any amount of exposure to air will dry it into an unusable brick. Once opened, wrap it up real tight—I like to press all the air out of the bag, roll it up, secure it with a rubber band, *then* stick it in a resealable plastic bag. You'll thank me later.

HONEY & MAPLE SYRUP

Both of these deserve a place in your cupboard (although, once opened, stick the maple syrup in the fridge). Look for "pure" on the packaging—some honey and maple syrups are corn syrup with added flavor and color. Use them to sweeten yogurt or oatmeal or to mellow the bite of a Dijon Vinaigrette (see page 60). They can be used in place of granulated sugar in whipped cream (see page 312) for delicate flavor and as a sugar substitute in most liquid preparations (like coffee or cocktails). Just know they will impart their unique high (floating like a honeybee) or low

> Try this for breakfast: Spread a piece of toast with tahini and top with a few slices of sweet-tart apple. Drizzle with honey and sprinkle with sesame seeds.

(rooted like a maple tree) notes wherever you add them.

BAKING POWDER, BAKING SODA, & VANILLA

If you've made chocolate chip cookies or other back-of-the-box recipes in the past year, you likely already have these around. I put them on the list as a reminder to check your stock. Baking powder and baking soda are both chemical leaveners; they make stuff rise and give most cakes, muffins, and biscuits their spring. They can lose their lift over time, though, so it's worth replacing them at least once a year. Pure vanilla extract adds its distinctive floral aroma and flavor to sweets and baked goods. Vanilla beans are great, and so is vanilla bean paste, but they can be expensive and harder to find. Use 'em if you got 'em.

CRACKERS OR CHIPS

As packaged, they make for great snacking or even emergency meals (see tinned fish on page 12). Crumbled, they add flavor and crunch to pie crusts, coatings, casserole or cassoulet toppings (see page 255) and can be used to bind meatballs or fritters in place of bread crumbs or flour. They're consistently preseasoned so you can add just a few to a recipe and it'll have a big impact. Look for salted or lightly salted options like saltines, Ritz (or other buttery rounds), and classic salted potato chips.

CHOCOLATE

You never know when a warm chocolate chip cookie (or warm chocolate cake or hot fudge sundae) craving might strike. A twelve-ounce bag of morsels is good. A few bars of good-quality baking chocolate is even better. In the recipes that follow, semisweet and bittersweet chocolate can be used interchangeably. Feel free to play around with ratios of milk to dark chocolate, as well, but remember that milk chocolate, because it's made with less naturally bitter-tasting cocoa, will add more sweetness to the finished product. Not that that's a bad thing. For a long time I had two large bags of fun-size Hershey bars in the pantry left over from a Halloween during which no trick-or-treaters showed up. Even these turned out to be a really lovely addition to the Brown Butter Chocolate Chip Cookies (see page 298).

> Speaking of candy bars, just about anything chocolate coated can be chopped and tossed into cookie dough in addition to or in place of chocolate chips.

DRIED FRUIT

Raisins can be polarizing, but they're not the only dried fruit on the market. Pick a few that you like and keep them stocked for folding into cookie or scone dough (see page 138), mixing into muffin batter, or shaking into GORP (that's Good Old Raisins & Peanuts). I like raisins, dried cherries, and dates (though dates are technically not dried). All are excellent natural sweeteners with the added benefit that, unlike sugar, they add unique flavor *and* texture. When pickled (see page 65) they soften and plump and lend bursts of acid and sweetness to crunchy salads, rich or meaty dishes like a roast chicken, or fried cutlets.

FLAKY SALT (OR FLEUR DE SEL)

These salts, with big, uneven crystals, add extra flavor, crunch, and a little sparkle to a dish. For flaky options look for Maldon sea salt flakes, available in most grocery stores, or Jacobsen Pure Flake Finishing Salt. French fleur de sel is slightly briny and evokes vacations on the Côte d'Azur (where I've never been but imagine is fabulous). I use these fancier salts as a counterpoint in rich dishes like a runny-yolked-Egg-in-a-Hole (see page 147), sweet things like the Magic Honey Sesame Sticks (see page 311), or to add crunch to carbs like potatoes. Lasts as long as it takes you to get through a bag, box, or tub.

DRIED CHILIES

Like their fresh counterparts, dried chilies lend heat, of course, but also unique floral and/or smoky qualities to sauces, broths, pastes, and other homemade spice blends and condiments. Even though they're dried, they should be flexible, not brittle. I like to add tiny chilies de árbol to beans and brothy soups. Use one, crushed between your fingers, anywhere a half teaspoon of crushed red pepper flakes are called for in a recipe. Guajillo, chipotle, and pasilla chilies are also fun varieties to play around with. I usually toast them in a hot cast-iron pan just until fragrant before soaking until soft and blending into braising liquids. Store these with other dried spices.

> I buy tuna labeled "pole and line caught" or "pole caught" and with the blue Marine Stewardship Council seal, two signs of an environmentally friendly choice.

TINNED FISH (TUNA, SARDINES, ANCHOVIES)

Tinned or canned fish is shelf stable, super flavorful, and, when it comes to oily varieties like sardines and mackerel, a heart-healthy and sustainable source of protein. Thoughtfully arranged on crackers or buttered toast and finished with a squeeze of lemon, they make a sophisticated hors d'oeuvre or a satisfying light meal (see the Tuna and Radish Toast, page 151). Add meatier types like tuna to pasta or a crunchy celery salad (see page 172). Sardines and anchovies can be assertive, but when used wisely, they add subtle salty flavor to a finished dish. Try sardines tossed with the Winter Pasta with Garlic, Olives, and Lemon (see page 228), or a few chopped anchovy fillets whisked into the Creamy Dressing base on page 62.

COCONUT MILK

Creamy, rich, and vegan to boot, canned coconut milk can be stirred into soups or a pot of beans, shaken into dressings, or blended into smoothies. The thick coconut cream that often separates in the can can even be whipped like heavy cream. Coconut milk's fat content is closer to heavy cream than milk, so feel free to use it anywhere heavy cream is suggested here—just don't forget it will make food taste like coconut. Be careful you're buying coconut *milk* and not coconut cream, which is super delicious but usually reserved for sweets and piña coladas.

CEREAL

Unsweetened cereal varieties—especially Rice Krispies and cornflake types—make fun additions to cookies (fold them in in place of or in addition to nuts), and add unexpected texture to homemade granola (see page 125). They can even be crushed and used to bread chicken (or fish or pork or whatever) cutlets.

THE FRIDGE

Keeping the refrigerator stocked with more than just jam and wine (or ketchup and beer) was one of my great leaps toward becoming a grown-up. The ingredients in cold storage—eggs, mustard, even milk—are the sometimes literal binders that bring meals together (see Freestyle Baked Pasta, page 235, milk; Oven-Baked Neatballs, page 96, eggs). I encourage you to maintain a strong awareness of your fridge inventory. It can look lean by the end of the week (or however long your shopping cycle is), but try not to let it go bare. That would force you to constantly shop from scratch, which can be expensive and inefficient. But if I have butter, Parmesan, and a box of pasta, I know I can come straight home and make dinner.

The whole point of cold storage is that it makes food last a lot longer. So stock your fridge not just with the fresh vegetables and herbs you know you'll get through in a week, but with longer-lasting items that can hang out for a season or two. Like these:

I am all for utility, but I buy special salted butter just for toast. Beurre de Baratte is my favorite (it's wrapped in gold foil and stamped with a picture of a cow—cute!), but Trader Joe's carries excellent and affordable French cultured butter, too.

UNSALTED BUTTER

The sweet cream flavor of unsalted butter is what gives cakes and cookies their unmistakable color, texture, and taste. Beat it at room temperature with sugar for light and tender-crumbed cakes, or melt it for something more dense and chewy like a fudgy brownie. A pat or two turns pan drippings from a seared steak into a silky sauce and transforms plain pasta into Cacio e Pepe. Just add pepper. Butter freezes beautifully, so buy in bulk when it's on sale (and if space permits). Also, never forget: it's good on toast.

EGGS

Keep large eggs on hand at all times to scramble, fry, poach, or bake into a frittata. Eggs are a cheap protein that can turn leftover vegetables and rice into a meal worth savoring. Most baking recipes call for (and work best with) large eggs. And size does matter—too much egg and you'll have a bouncy, overrisen cake or cookie. Too small and you won't get enough lift. But if you're just scrambling, buy whichever size you like.

DIJON AND/OR WHOLE-GRAIN MUSTARD

More Dijon than seems right is the secret to my Dijon Vinaigrette (see page 60). A dollop evens out the richness of mac and cheese, and gives a little oomph to burgers and meat loaf. It's salty, tangy, and slightly spicy—three elements that most dishes and dressings desperately need. Opt for Maille or Grey Poupon if you can.

FULL-FAT PLAIN YOGURT AND/OR SOUR CREAM

A big spoonful of one of these is the key to fluffy frittatas and ultramoist cakes (see page 297). Fold in a handful of chopped herbs or caramelized onions for an irresistible dip, spread it on plates below spice-dusted grilled meats, or serve on top of spicy dishes like curries or chili. Rarely have I encountered yogurt or sour cream that has gone bad, but they can get quite a bit tangier the longer they sit around. Taste and adjust seasonings accordingly.

KETCHUP

Sweet, salty, tangy, umami, ketchup is one of the great wonders of the condiment world. I keep ketchup around for frozen french fries and hot dogs, but I also squeeze it into recipes when I'm out of tomato paste and use it to make a little dip for a few leftover shrimp or a spread for a ham-and-cheese sandwich (see page 83). Got kids? Reason enough. I like Heinz.

JAM, OR MARMALADE

While I really like to make my own jam (see page 86), I always back up with a jar of store-bought preserves. And not just because we eat a lot of PB and J in my house. Fruit spreads of all flavors can add sheen to glazed chicken or tofu, lend balance to a salty sauce, or make an easy tart filling (see page 307). You know what flavors you prefer, so buy those, but I'm partial to apricot preserves and orange marmalade.

MAYONNAISE

Even if you don't take mayonnaise on your turkey and Swiss, you should keep it in your pantry. Start to think of it as an ingredient and not just a condiment. Use it in place of butter when making a grilled cheese. It has a higher smoke point than butter, so you can cook your sandwich longer for a more deeply golden crust and melted cheese. Fold it into creamy dips and dressings for body and balance against tangy ingredients like sour cream and yogurt, or stir in some chopped garlic and a squeeze of lemon juice for an elevated aioli (see page 83). I'll never understand why mayo is sold in the middle of the supermarket when, once opened, it lives in the refrigerator. Still, refrigerate after opening.

MILK AND/OR NONDAIRY ALTERNATIVES

I am not a milk drinker, but I always have at least a quart of whole milk in the fridge for baking or cooling off oatmeal. I prefer to use whole milk, but feel free to use whatever you regularly buy, even almond, oat, or coconut milk, wherever cow's milk is called for in these pages (just avoid anything flavored). To be safe, abide by the expiration date, but you often have a day or three after that until it turns. Give it a sniff and a tiny taste to be sure.

SOY SAUCE

Soy sauce, shoyu (Japanese-style soy sauce), and gluten-free tamari add more than saltiness to food: just a tablespoon gives complexity to brothy soups, braises, dressings, and marinades—it's even a secret ingredient in my Thanksgiving

It's Hellmann's all the way for me.

gravy. Anywhere I use soy sauce or tamari, I still season with a little salt to enhance its flavor. I use regular soy sauce and the like in my recipes, but low-sodium options work, too, if that's what you have.

HOT STUFF

Hot sauces aren't just hot, they're often tangy and/or sweet and/or kinda funky depending on what else they're made with. Jing Gao, creator of Fly By Jing, a line of Sichuan sauces and spices, points out that ingredients like dried mushrooms, brown sugar, nuts, and sesame oil can adjust the flavor, fragrance, and mouth feel of Chinese chili oils and sauces. Whatever hot topper you choose, consider what you're eating and season accordingly. Try slightly sweet Sriracha on an egg sandwich, Indonesian sambal stirred into a soy-based salad dressing, and chopped Calabrian chilies dribbled over spaghetti. Gao even spoons her Sichuan Chili Crisp over vanilla ice cream for a sweet and spicy treat (try it!).

For more thoughts on hots, see page 69.

OLIVES OR CAPERS

Briny olives and capers are two more ingredients that add flavor but require no work from you. If you're olive-averse, try Castelvetrano olives—they're mild. Likewise, I find salt-packed capers to be a little easier on the palate than their vinegar-packed counterparts (but give them a rinse before using). Chop them up when you want to add extra zing to salad dressings (see page 62), or fold them into tuna with lemon and a little olive oil. Or combine them with onions, garlic, a handful of herbs and a sprinkle of Parmesan for the Winter Pasta with Garlic, Olives, and Lemon on page 228.

PARMESAN AND/OR PECORINO ROMANO

If you keep one cheese only in your deli drawer, I think it should be Parmesan. Look for Parmigiano Reggiano, the gold standard of Parmesan cheeses. It's slightly pricier than domestic options but totally worth it. It melts, albeit slowly, and it packs a salty, nutty punch that other widely available cheeses lack. Use it to amp up a grilled cheese, grate over a bowl of warm pasta, or bake into a crispy salad topping (see page 46). Shop for a hunk of Parm with some rind attached; when you're done with the cheese part, drop the rind into stock or sauce to infuse them with dazzling umami flavor. Pecorino Romano, a hard sheep's milk cheese, is another good pasta topper. It's a little saltier and tangier than Parmesan, so dust lightly to start. I keep both around, but either will work where Parmesan is called for.

A NICE MELTING CHEESE

I know I just said you could get away with Parmesan alone, but—and this may be because I have little kids—I am never without a pound of sharp white cheddar cheese. It melts beautifully between two slices of buttered bread, atop tuna salad (controversial, I know), or tucked inside a tortilla. It can also stand in for mozzarella in a baked pasta. Even unmelted, slices of it are welcome with crackers or shaved into salads of all kinds. Other good melters include Gruyère (love), Provolone (yep), and Monterey Jack (sure, why not).

CURED MEATS

Packed with the intense flavors of pork, salt, and sometimes spices (check those labels), pancetta, bacon, chorizo, and the like are valuable additions to your pantry. As the meat cooks in a hot skillet, its flavorful fat melts. Use that to cook with in place of or in addition to oil. Think an egg fried in bacon drippings. Cured meats should last several weeks if not longer in the refrigerator, but if they get slimy or funky before you have a chance to use them, it's time to restock.

CITRUS

Nothing compares to the bright flavors that citrus adds to a dish. I always have lemons and limes in the fridge, and come winter, when they're at their best, oranges and grapefruits, too. A squeeze of lemon can freshen everything from a glass of water to a bowl of pasta. Or chop the whole thing up, rind and all, and add it to frozen peas (see page 179). Limes can dress up a taco (see page 259) or a bowl of fried rice. I like oranges and grapefruits layered into salads (see page 174) and squeezed into a refreshing homemade soda (see page 288).

HEARTY VEGETABLES

Carrots and celery last a really long time and have many uses. They can be eaten raw or cooked, and even turn water into stock with an assist from onions. Broccoli, kale, collards, cabbage, and the like can last a really long time in the fridge as well. If you have the stamina to wash and dry your leafy greens when you get home from the store, do it. When kept dry and loosely sealed in a plastic bag, these stay ready for long or quick-cooking (see page 74) and salading (see page 161) for a couple of weeks.

FRESH HERBS

Get in the habit of keeping one or two types of fresh herbs in the crisper. I vote for flat-leaf Italian parsley plus another of your choice. (If forced to pick a number two, I'd say cilantro, though it should be noted that to some people, cilantro tastes like soap due to a genetic reason I can't explain here. If that's the case with you, how about mint?) Next to lemons or vinegar, herbs are the easiest way to add bright flavors to a recipe. Worried you won't get through the bunch? There are lots of smart ways to use them up, like pestos (see page 99), sauces (see page 76), pasta (see page 228), and salads (see page 162). To store, wash, and spin dry, spread them out on a few sheets of connected paper towels, roll up loosely, and stick inside a resealable plastic bag or other container. They'll last you a week or so.

GHEE OR COCONUT OIL

Most commonly found in Indian cuisine, ghee is a type of clarified butter often made from cultured dairy. Its rich, nutty flavor and high smoke point make it a delicious alternative to vegetable oil for frying rice, sautéing vegetables, or as a base for curries. Same goes for coconut oil. Use it for high-heat cooking where you want a bit of added flavor, especially to fry tofu or add oomph to vegan soups or stews. Both taste delicious when used to pop stovetop popcorn

FRESH GINGER

I don't always have ginger in my fridge, but when I do it ends up in everything: salad dressings (see page 62), soups (see page 217), and my favorite curried beans (see page 211). It can play both sweet and savory, and sliced, chopped, or grated, it adds distinct heat and aroma wherever you use it. Keep it dry and store in the crisper. If your ginger's on the edge of going bad, slice it and cover with boiling water and let it steep for ten minutes. Strain, add a little honey, a squeeze of lemon, and a pinch of cayenne for an instant cold remedy.

HEAVY CREAM

Heavy cream is a special-occasion item for me—birthdays, holiday baking, chocolate sauce making, etc. You can add a splash to enrich soups or finish a simple pasta, but I tend to use it mostly to make whipped cream (see page 312). I like mine whipped to soft peaks (when you lift the whisk, the cream should bend like a ballerina taking her bow—I don't remember where I heard that, but it's nice, isn't it?) and I sweeten it very lightly if at all. About a tablespoon of sweetener—powdered, granulated, or brown sugar; maple syrup or honey—to one cup cream is a reliable ratio.

KIMCHI & SAUERKRAUT

What I like most about kimchi and sauerkraut—besides the naturally occurring good-for-you probiotics—is how they add instant salt, tang, and sometimes heat wherever you use them. My dear friend Nancy's mom, Angela, makes her own kimchi about every six weeks. She eats it with most meals, but my favorite is as an addition to Frank Cha's Special Ramen, Nancy's dad's Christmas Day offering. Store bought or homemade, you can fold kimchi into an omelet, tuck it into a grilled cheese, or chop it and blend with cream cheese to serve with crackers. Sauerkraut, too, plays nice with melted cheese. Sandwich in a quesadilla (see page 156), serve with meaty sausages or, you know, on top of hot dogs.

MISO PASTE

This thick, salty paste is made from fermented soybeans and sometimes rice and other grains. It comes in white, yellow, and red. I like white miso because it has the mildest flavor and is slightly sweet. Yellow miso, made with barley and sometimes rice, is a bit stronger in flavor but still mild enough for all-purpose uses like quick soups or whisking into dressings. Because it's fermented, miso contains good-for-you bacteria. In her book, *Japanese Home Cooking*, author Sonoko Sakai calls miso a "living seasoning." It's heat sensitive, though, so once it's added, turn off the heat. Keep it refrigerated and it should last you at least a year.

WINE

For drinking. Oh, more? A splash also adds acid and sweetness to long-cooked items like the 53-Minute Ragu on page 91 or the Braised Beef with Tomatoes and Onions on page 247.

For the simplest miso soup, my friend writer Sanaë Lemoine's Japanese mother recommends a teaspoon or two of miso stirred into a cup of hot water; top with a little sliced scallion.

THE FREEZER

Keep the right things on ice and you'll find your freezer can be a treasure trove of dinner (or dessert) solutions. The only thing you need to negotiate is defrosting time. Speed up the process by soaking frozen items, particularly meat or fish, in a tightly sealed bag in a bowl of cold water. You'll decrease defrost time by at least half a day. Otherwise, defrost according to package directions, or if you're still not sure, in the fridge overnight.

FROZEN VEGETABLES

I prefer to stock spinach, peas, and corn, but it's smart to keep a couple of bags of whatever frozen vegetables you prefer on hand. I stress that you buy those you like and will actually eat, because even I have found that half-eaten bag of emergency veggie medley wedged in the back of my freezer. Toss into pastas, simmer in soups, or dress them up with frizzled onions and lemon (see page 179).

FROZEN FRUIT

I love (when someone makes me) a frozen fruit smoothie on a Saturday morning, but I also like a handful of berries in muffins, quick breads, and cakes. You can even spin frozen fruit into a no-churn sorbet (see page 295) or cook it down to make your own jam (see page 86). Freezer space can get tight, though, so know your own habits—if you'll use frozen fruit, stock up; if not, skip it for one of the other items on the list.

SAUSAGES

I keep several links of frozen sweet or hot Italian sausage wrapped tightly in plastic in packs of two, stashed in a resealable plastic bag. They're freezer friendly because they're relatively high in fat, so they won't dry out once defrosted. When you're ready to roast, grill, or use in a stew, grab as many links as you need and defrost overnight in the fridge or sink them, still wrapped and in a tightly sealed bag, in a bowlful of cold water (that'll take about an hour).

SHRIMP

Keep a pound or two of large, wild-caught shrimp in the freezer and you're minutes away from dinner any night of the week. Buying frozen means the shrimp wait for you rather than the ones you buy "previously frozen"—those require immediate attention. When you're ready to rock, toss the shrimp into a colander set inside a big bowl and rinse under cold water until they're defrosted (about ten minutes). Peel if necessary and pat dry before using. Sauté with chorizo (see page 240), or sear and toss with garlic and butter, or steam and eat with aioli (see page 83) for dipping.

FISH FILLETS

Unless you live by the sea, I recommend you buy frozen fish. Most frozen fish hits the deep freeze right on the boat where it's caught, ensuring its quality stays top-notch and that it gets labeled appropriately. Plus, frozen fish is often

I like to defrost frozen fish right before I'm going to cook it: Place it in a resealable plastic bag and set in a bowl full of cold water. Takes about 15 minutes.

25

more affordable than fresh options. And there's no need to panic if you bought fish on the way home from work and decided upon checkout that you needed a pizza instead. Frozen salmon and cod fillets are pretty easy to find in well-stocked supermarkets. They usually come individually frozen in four- to six-ounce portions, so you can pull out as many fillets as people you're feeding.

POTATOES (TOTS, WAFFLE FRIES, OR SIMILAR)

Wild card! Keeping crunchy spuds in the freezer means I can round out burger night or dress down a semifancy fish dish for the kiddos in a snap. I don't make tots or waffle fries nearly as often as I think about it, but having them in the freezer feels a little like having the answers in the back of the book. You don't *need* them, per se, but they can sure be useful.

NUTS, SEEDS, & COCONUT

Nuts can be pricey, which is why I buy them in bulk and keep them in the freezer. They are full of natural oils, so they can go rancid quickly if not stored in a cool place. Sticking them in the freezer lengthens their shelf life and likely saves you some coin. I stock a variety of nuts and seeds for dressing up oatmeal, adding crunch to salads, or just snacking out of hand. Keep unsweetened coconut flakes and chips in the freezer as well and they'll last a really long time.

BREAD

Whether you buy or bake your own loaves, slice and store your bread in the freezer after a day or two. Yes, it lives here. Because here it lives indefinitely. You'll always have toast at the ready, plus options for sandwiches, French toast, and the ever-important crouton (see page 46). Also, when I say "bread," I mean breadlike things. After a couple of days split and store bagels, English muffins, even pita in the freezer. Defrost in the toaster or, in the case of pita or the flatbreads on page 107, the microwave for about 22 seconds.

OTHER MEAT & CHICKEN

I prefer to buy my animal proteins closer to when I want to cook them, mostly because my freezer is pretty well stocked (see page 25), and keeping meat in there takes up a lot of room. That said, if something I use often, like grass-fed ground beef or chicken thighs is on sale, I'll buy twice what I came for and stick half in the freezer. The only trick is defrosting time—it can vary wildly. Best bet, take frozen meat out of the freezer and put in the fridge the night before you plan to cook it. If you're a couple of hours out from cooking and it's still not defrosted, set it on the counter. The USDA would probably frown upon this, but I do it, my mom did it, and I think you can do it, too.

ICE CREAM

In a cup or on a cone, atop warm cake or all alone. Ice cream, like Sandra Boynton, is on regular rotation in our house. Let it soften slightly and swirl with sorbet (see page 291), sandwich between cookies (see page 298), or let it melt until soupy and use it like a fancy (but secretly easy) dessert sauce for fresh or frozen berries.

HOW TO ORGANIZE IT

Now that you have a beautifully stocked pantry full of ingredients, it's time to organize it. I don't want to get too prescriptive, because a lot of pantry organization depends on the specific structure of your kitchen. Some might have walk-in pantries with shelves on three sides, while others keep the bakeware in the oven just to free up an extra cupboard for canned goods. You'll figure out where exactly to store things, but there are a few good rules to keep in mind that will help you stay way more organized.

Important note: I am not by nature a superorganized, type-A person. It's only out of necessity (work, two wee babes, wanting to have a life outside of the kitchen) that I've learned to keep and maintain a tidy pantry. If I can do it, so can you. The following "rules" are really just what I refer to as "keeping one's head out of one's ass." We all need reminding sometimes.

CUPBOARD

KEEP LIKE WITH LIKE

It goes without saying (I hope) that you should keep refrigerated and frozen items in the designated areas. More on that in a sec. Dry goods, however, can require a little more thinking. Next time you go to the grocery store, take a look at those aisle markers overhead. See how all the baking stuff is in one place together? And all the canned goods? It's not just because it makes logical sense. It's also a smart and efficient use of space. Use this as your inspiration. Not only will your brain look for like items near one another, but cans stack neatly on top of each other; bags of flour and sugar have

similar sizes and shapes. Group like and similarly packaged items together to maximize space. Also consider the weight of things. Keep oft-used and heavier items on lower shelves for easy access and to reduce shelf sag.

DON'T DECANT

For a time I was convinced that decanting was the way to go. That way, I could display charming jars of rice, pasta, and cereal right on the counter. But now that I have a grown-up coffeemaker and sippy cups to drip-dry, I'm not willing to give up that kind of real estate. Plus my containers are never quite big enough to fit an entire bag of flour or whatever. I ended up with both full containers and nearly empty bags in the pantry. Instead, keep ingredients in their original containers.

It saves you time, space, and helps you keep track of exactly how much you have left. That said, I recently moved and now cook in a kitchen with easily accessible open shelving right above the sink. So I have decanted my rice and grains to make things fit. (The alternative spot was our repurposed coat closet with a rolling cart, and that's for cookie supplies.) The above advice is still my best, but make adjustments to suit your own space.

AVOID OVERFLOW

Unless you're feeding more than three professional athletes with huge appetites on a regular basis or live more than twenty-five miles from your nearest supermarket, I don't recommend auxiliary storage. In my opinion, this encourages hoarding and keeps you from taking a hard look at what you're really cooking and eating on a regular basis. If food is out of sight (in the garage or basement, for example), it's likely out of mind.

FRIDGE
ADJUST YOUR SHELVES

Some fridge storage is self-explanatory: i.e., condiments fit nicely in those door compartments; fruits and vegetables generally go in the crisper drawers. Otherwise, like your cupboard, much depends on the design of your refrigerator itself. I find tall, skinny fridges (the ones that are side by side with the freezer) the most challenging to organize. A reminder, though, that you don't have to stand in front of the fridge yelling at the milk to *get in there!*—you can adjust those shelves to suit your needs.

KEEP THINGS IN PLAIN SIGHT

There are lots of articles on the Internet that tell you where *not* to put the milk or eggs for fear of spoilage. But I can say after years of absentmindedly tossing things into the fridge—at home and at work—that a slight temperature fluctuation inside the refrigerator is not what causes food to go bad. Food spoils (at least in my experience) because I forget about it or because I'm not honest with myself about what I eat. Cravings fluctuate of course, but if you can't seem to get through the half gallon of milk before it starts to smell sour, try buying a smaller size—even better, buy shelf stable milk cartons (sold near the juice boxes). They're great for baking or using in coffee and last a lot longer than the refrigerated stuff.

The best guidance I can offer when it comes to organizing your refrigerator is to keep things in plain sight. I can't tell you how many times I've forgotten about a leftover because it was in a short container hiding behind a big yogurt. Opt for clear storage containers that either stack comfortably on top of one another or are tall enough to see if stuck in the back. Oh, and keep any raw meat on the bottom shelf, preferably on a rimmed plate or baking sheet, lest it leaks on anything fresh.

FREEZER

YOUR MODEL MATTERS

I have had all kinds of freezers in my life. Tiny frosted-over iceboxes in my studio apartment, deep pull-out drawers in my first grown-up place, and a narrow stand-up in my current residence. I grew up with the freezer on top of the fridge design and I still find it the easiest to organize. If this is your model and it doesn't come with a shelf (one of my rental freezers did not), you can buy portable shelf inserts from the Container Store or similar storage retailers to add more surface area on which to stack.

The tall, skinny freezer is my second favorite—its many shelves make it easy to group like items together (bags of frozen fruits or vegetables; proteins; ice cream) and is by far the easiest to access. But you can't fit a baking sheet inside—tough for holiday cookie prep and baking, of which I do a lot.

Then there are the big drawer freezers. Appealing at first—they're *so big*—they become a challenge once well stocked. The nuts are buried under the peas under the breast milk or what have you. Unless you are a master "flat freezer" (that is, you transfer all your liquid preparations to a resealable plastic bag, freeze flat, then stack—who has the time or wants to use that many gallon bags?), it can be challenging to keep track of things. To make it slightly easier, label items so you can identify them easily from the top down.

HOW TO MAINTAIN IT

STORE SMART

Even in the most pristine homes where I worked as a private chef, there was a drawer of jumbled plastic storage containers. It is, like jury duty and the DMV, one of life's great equalizers. Commit to clear storage containers for, well, everything. Glass is great, but it can get heavy, especially if you want to pack your lunch in it. I like reusable lightweight plastic (BPA-free of course).

I've found no better option than the restaurant and test-kitchen standard-issue

plastic "deli containers with lids" (that's how they're usually sold, and if you google that phrase they will show up). They come in cup, pint, and quart sizes and they all take the same lids. No numbering bottoms and tops, no newfangled organizational systems. I wouldn't microwave in them (hot plastic makes me nervous), but they can go on the top rack of the dishwasher.

SEAL 'EM UP

Treated with respect, pantry items should last a really long time. That's the point. But proper storage and a tight seal is key to an ingredient's long, happy life. How many times have you gone to make chocolate chip cookies only to find an opened box of brown sugar that's hard as a brick? Do your best to roll bags up tightly and secure them with a chip clip or a good old rubber band. *Even if those bags are already in a box.* For extra protection, toss more vulnerable items (the brown sugar, things that will sog in humid environs) in a resealable plastic bag or one of those large deli containers.

LABEL IT

This mostly applies to items stored in the freezer, but it's a good habit to get into with anything you make ahead. Keep a little roll of tape (Scotch or masking is fine) and a Sharpie in a drawer or pencil caddy in the kitchen. Simply write what's in the container and when you made it, and you'll never have to wonder what those gravy-colored ice blocks are again.

FIRST IN, FIRST OUT

Maybe the most important thing they teach you in cooking school (I mean, besides the cooking part) is the rule of FIFO: first in, first out. Whatever you bought first, use first. Whatever you made first, eat first, etc.

CHECK IN

Once a week—or whenever you think about it—give the fridge and freezer a quick once-over. Plan to cook ingredients on their last legs ASAP and throw away (or compost/rinse and recycle) anything past its prime.

You'll soon start to notice your own patterns, and the guilt of throwing away unused food should be enough to keep you from buying (or making) anything you just don't use.

A NOSE KNOWS

In most cases, expiration and sell-by dates are a little loosey-goosey. You usually have three to five days post-date to get through, say, the yogurt or half box of chicken stock. Some ingredients make it very clear when they're ready to get tossed—for example, mold or fizzy bubbles (which indicate fermentation has started; fine in sauerkraut, not cool in salsa). But don't forget that your "nose knows." Take a sniff: Sour? Funky? Musty? Probably time to go. Trust your gut and when in doubt, throw it out.

EQUIPMENT

I have cooked in many home kitchens, both humble and high-test, and the one thing I can attest to is that you don't need a ton of stuff. Just the right stuff. I don't believe in keeping lots of tools and equipment around because, honestly, I don't have the space to store them. As is the case with your pantry, the more you cook, the more you'll realize what you can't live without, what you can donate, and what you need to keep around for holiday baking or nostalgia's sake. I cannot seem to part with my mini madeleine pans. Can't tell you who gave them to me or when I used them last, but they are too precious to part with. This streamlined list is what I can't cook without.

CUTTING BOARDS

I like to use a **big, heavy** wooden board for the bulk of my prep. Good boards can be costly, but there's nothing scarier than trying to chop on a wobbly surface. If your board is wiggly, place a slightly damp dish towel (or a few barely damp paper towels) underneath. This should keep the board in place. I also keep a lighter weight plastic board around for dealing with raw meat or seafood or odorous things like onions and garlic. That way I can stick it in the dishwasher to make sure it gets superhot and sanitized. I understand the impulse to keep a hefty wooden board for everything, but it is very sad to bite into a scallion-scented strawberry.

KNIVES, A FEW

CHEF'S KNIFE

You'll use this most. I don't care what brand you buy. The important thing is that it's comfortable in your hand. I have weak wrists, so I like a lightweight knife (Victorinox makes a reliable line with thin blades and plastic handles). Once you find a chef's knife you like, keep it sharp. Depending on how often you cook, you should probably get your knives professionally sharpened a couple of times a year. Wash them by hand. They get knocked around in the dishwasher, which dulls blades.

SERRATED KNIFE

For slicing through crusty loaves of bread, crumb-topped cakes, and tender fruits like tomatoes. Look for one with an offset blade, which prevents your knuckles from dragging across the cutting board.

> Remember: A sharp knife is safer than a dull one. A dull blade requires more of your muscle, so if you slip, it has that much more force behind it. Keep blades sharp and out of reach of little hands.

PARING KNIFE

Use these small knives for detail work like hulling strawberries, halving grapes, or other baby and toddler preparations. Also useful for tightening that teeny-tiny screw on your glasses.

SKILLETS

CAST-IRON

When treated right, cast iron can last lifetimes. Yes, that's plural. If you didn't inherit one from your grandma, Lodge makes durable, affordable, preseasoned skillets. I have lots of friends who have picked these up at estate sales as well, though those often need a little TLC to get them back up and running. (Google "Kat Kinsman cast iron." You'll be impressed.) I recommend one with a ten- or twelve-inch diameter. I own a ten-inch-pan and only sometimes do I wish it were slightly bigger. Though I assume when my kids are older with bigger appetites I'll want to size up. The big benefit is that cast iron gets hot and stays consistently hot, so you don't have to fiddle with the heat too much. Debate rages over cast-iron cleaning methods, but I clean mine with soap and water. Then, instead of leaving it to dry in the rack, I place the skillet back on the stove over medium heat until all the water evaporates. I turn off the heat and wipe the inside of the skillet with a paper towel dipped in a little vegetable oil. Leave it on the stovetop to cool completely (but cover that handle with an oven mitt so no one gets burned).

LARGE STAINLESS STEEL

I have a big twelve-inch-wide stainless steel skillet that I love for shallow braises like chicken thighs. This is also where I make most of my pasta sauces so I can add the noodles straight into that pan with a little pasta water. That way I can toss, toss, toss, with plenty of room, as the liquid reduces and coats the pasta to luscious perfection.

NONSTICK

I cook all my eggs in a nonstick skillet, and my fish, too. I think you only need one, and a ten-inch-pan should do for singles or couples; twelve inches for families of four or more.

POTS

BIG DUTCH OVEN OR SIMILAR HEAVY-BOTTOMED POT

These are best for soups, stews, braising meats, and boiling pasta. Most enamel Dutch ovens and stainless steel pots can go from stovetop to oven; just be aware of any plastic parts on the handles or knobs that could melt at high temperatures. These days, most decent cookware—say from Staub, Le Creuset, or Great Jones—can take the heat.

MEDIUM POT

I use a stainless steel medium pot (that's four- or five-quart capacity) most frequently after my cast-iron skillet. You can pull off a small batch of marinara in here, boil all your grains, make oatmeal, and the like. All your pots should feel kind of heavy for their size, which will keep food from scorching on the bottom over high heat.

SMALL POT

If you are cooking for one or two, a small pot could replace your medium one. I don't use it nearly as often as my big or medium pots, but it's nice to have if I'm reheating soup or other brothy items just for me.

BAKING

BAKING SHEETS

Ideally you'll have a couple of sturdy, rimmed, 18-by-13-inch sheets with about a one-inch rim. Search "rimmed baking sheets" and these will pop right up. Use them for roasting meat and potatoes and baking cookies; you can even roast a whole turkey on one. If all you have is a jelly roll pan (which is the technical term for smaller rimmed baking sheets at about 10½-by-15½ inches used to make old-school rolled cakes), that's OK, too.

BAKING VESSELS

A two-quart (8-by-8-inch square) and a three-quart (9-by-13-inch) ought to keep you in business. For cakes and bars and the like, I prefer pans with straight, rather than sloped, sides, but that's a personal preference. Pyrex still makes dependable bakeware in a variety of sizes and shapes.

OTHER EQUIPMENT

TIMER

I am easily distracted, in life and in the kitchen. "Scorch of the day!" we used to call it when the smell of bitter burning foodstuffs called me back to task: the blackened nuts, the stuck-on tomato sauce, the carbonized scones. Setting a timer will save you every time. Do I forget to set it sometimes? You bet. But every time I do remember, man am I grateful. You can certainly use the timer on your phone, but I prefer one with an annoying beep that I can keep on or near the fridge. That way I'm forced to return to the kitchen to turn it off. Usually in the nick of time.

TONGS

Think of these as an extension of your arm. They keep your precious hands at a distance from hot stuff. Tongs make it easy to grab and turn big pieces of meat in the oven, on the stove, or on the grill. Also good for grabbing lightweight items off of high shelves. Test tongs with a few squeezes before buying. The tension should feel comfortable; you shouldn't have to work too hard.

WHISK

You probably have one, which is great, but in most cases you can use a fork.

WOODEN SPOON

When I say, "Cook, stirring occasionally," I envision you using a wooden spoon. They're lightweight, durable, and won't scrape up the bottoms of pots and pans.

Y PEELER

You likely have a vegetable peeler already, but if you're in the market, Kuhn Rikon makes a hard-wearing, inexpensive little peeler perfect for stripping potatoes, carrots, or citrus.

MICROPLANE ZESTER

I'm not one to recommend brand names—Oh wait, I guess I am (see almost every page previous to this one) but the Microplane Classic Zester can't be beat. Use it to zest citrus and grate garlic, hard cheeses, or whole nutmeg.

RUBBER SPATULA

For gently scraping every last smear of batter or dough from bowls. Silicone versions are impervious to heat so can be used for stovetop cooking as well.

THE OTHER KIND OF SPATULA

Sometimes called a pancake turner, this spatula can be used to flip stuff over or transfer things from skillet to rack or baking sheet to plate. If you're in the market, I recommend a fish spatula. It has a long, thin, slightly flexible surface that easily slips under fritters, pancakes, cookies, and yes, fish fillets.

SALAD SPINNER

There is no easier way to wash lettuce and herbs than in a salad spinner. Here's how: place the leaves in the basket of the spinner inside the bowl (try not to fill more than halfway). Fill the bowl with cold water all the way to the top. Swish the leaves around and wait a few minutes to let any dirt or grit fall to the bottom of the bowl. Lift the basket out of the bowl, then dump out the dirty water (or use to water a plant). Return the basket with leaves to the bowl and spin dry. Repeat as necessary until leaves are squeaky clean. Spread whatever you washed in a single layer on a few sheets of connected paper towels and roll up. Store loosely, still in those paper towels, in a resealable bag.

MACHINES

I tend to reject machines in the kitchen. Most of those robots take up far more real estate than I can afford to give up. That said, for baking I like an **electric mixer**—handheld or stand is fine. Then there's the question of **blender** or **food processor**. I find that if you have one, you usually have the other, but if you're outfitting a new kitchen and want to ask for one for a birthday or something, I say go with a food processor. Almost anything you can do in a blender, you can do in a food processor.

All that aside, I've often said that when the apocalypse comes and we hit the road, I'm only taking a lighter and my cast-iron pan.

39

PART 2

WHAT TO MAKE

Now that your store-bought pantry is ready to go, it's time to set yourself up for success. Building a collection of homemade staples—your Pantry+ Ingredients— keeps fast and easy cooking from getting boring.

WHAT'S A PANTRY+ INGREDIENT ANYWAY?

In this section, you'll find what my friend Mollie calls "jazzy extras"—finishing touches that amp up the flavor and appearance of potentially plain, everyday dishes. What's extra cool is that all the Pantry+ ingredients in this section are made from and add to your existing store-bought stash. Think homemade croutons from leftover bread; salad dressings made with simple essentials; two sauces from canned tomatoes and onions.

You don't need *all* of these Pantry+ ingredients on hand *all* the time, but having a few prepared will help deliver big, craveable flavors without a ton of effort. Some of these staples are close to complete dishes all by themselves (a meaty ragu, a sultry pot of beans). Add pasta or toast and dinner's done. Others are fun finishing touches, which you can use to dress up dishes in your regular rotation—pesto (page 99) on grilled cheese; Zing! Sauce (page 82) on rice, toasted seeds on a simple salad. Both make meals taste like I worked much harder and much longer on them than I did. I know they'll do the same for you.

Cooked bacon is its own special flourish. To cook: Arrange in a single layer on a rimmed baking sheet and bake at 400°F until crisp, 15 to 20 minutes.

IN THE CUPBOARD
CRUNCHIES

We eat a lot of bread and breadlike products in our house—sourdough boules, English muffins, bagels, sliced sandwich bread: no loaf left behind! We often have a random assortment of bread butts that three out of four family members reject. And I can only eat so many myself. In an effort to curb our waste, I stash these odds and ends in the freezer until I have a few cups. Then I tear them up, douse them all in olive oil, and bake them until crunchy—and irresistible once again.

When you're cooking fast and easy, it's tempting to race to the finish line, plunk down a plate of steamed vegetables or sautéed greens, and expect everyone—including yourself—to get down with gusto. But it can be sad to fork down a plate of "simply steamed" anything. Shower it with crushed croutons, though? Boom! It's a recipe. Sprinkle it with flavorful toasted seeds? I'll have seconds. Or gild the lily and scatter bits of crisped Parmesan over a bowl of buttered noodles.

The crunchies on the following pages add instant interest and flavor to even the most straightforward preparation. I use croutons on salads of course (Spicy Lemon Chicken Salad, page 219), but I also crush them up and use them in place of panko (Shrimp and Chorizo

with Crushed Croutons, page 240) and fold them into meatballs in place of bread crumbs (page 96). Try the Mixed Seed Sprinkle (page 47) over a halved avocado or a salad, the Coconut Crunch (page 47) over roasted vegetables or greens. The Cheese Crispies (page 46) are pretty good on anything savory (float them atop your next Opportunity Soup, page 268). The same goes for the Garlic-Shallot Crunch (page 48). Just a tablespoon or two of these crunchies are enough to make a plain bowl of steamed rice really sing.

A reminder (if you skipped the intro) that you don't have to make and keep all of these crunchies around all of the time. Even having just one of them at the ready can set you up for a delicious meal. I suggest starting with the croutons.

OIL & HERB CROUTONS

COCONUT CRUNCH

GARLIC-SHALLOT CRUNCH

CHEESE CRISPIES

MIXED SEED SPRINKLE

OIL & HERB CROUTONS

Active time: 10 minutes | Total time: 50 minutes | Makes about 4 cups

These homemade croutons are good to go right off the baking sheet, but they get even better over time. Stored in an airtight container, they absorb the aromas of the garlic and herbs—making them even more flavorful. But they're pretty great with just olive oil and salt if that's all you have.

8 ounces bread, torn into bite-size pieces (about 4 cups)

⅓ cup olive oil

2 garlic cloves, smashed and peeled

4 sprigs fresh thyme, oregano, or rosemary or 1 teaspoon dried thyme or oregano

1 teaspoon kosher salt

Freshly ground black pepper

Preheat the oven to 300°F. On a rimmed baking sheet, toss the bread with the oil, garlic, thyme, salt, and several grinds of black pepper.

Bake, shaking the baking sheet halfway through, until the croutons are dry and golden brown, 30 to 35 minutes. Let cool completely before storing. Croutons will keep in an airtight container at room temperature up to 1 month.

CHEESE CRISPIES

Active time: 5 minutes | Total time: 20 minutes | Makes about 1½ cups

Use the small holes of a box grater to finely grate the cheese for these—preferably not a Microplane, which makes too fluffy a cheese pile for this application.

4 ounces Parmesan or sharp cheddar cheese, finely grated (about 1 cup)

Freshly ground black pepper

Preheat the oven to 375°F. Line a baking sheet with parchment paper. Spread the Parmesan in an even layer on the prepared sheet and top with a few grinds of black pepper. Bake until golden and bubbly, 10 to 12 minutes. Let cool completely, then break into pieces. Crispies will keep in an airtight container at room temperature up to 3 weeks.

COCONUT CRUNCH

Active time: 5 minutes | Total time: 10 minutes | Makes 1 cup

I have burned a lot of coconut in my day. I understand the impulse to just throw it in the oven at 375°F and move on. But don't rush. If the oven's too hot or you're not paying attention, coconut chips can go from golden brown to burned to a crisp in half a minute. Seasoned or not, when baked at 300°F, they'll be perfectly toasted every time.

1 cup coconut chips

½ teaspoon kosher salt

½ teaspoon sweet paprika

½ teaspoon sugar, optional

Preheat the oven to 300°F. Toss the coconut with the salt, paprika, and sugar, if using, in a large bowl. Spread on a rimmed baking sheet and bake until the color of cornflakes, 5 to 7 minutes. Let cool completely before storing. Coconut crunch will keep in an airtight container at room temperature up to 3 months.

MIXED SEED SPRINKLE

Active time: 5 minutes | Total time: 5 minutes | Makes about ⅓ cup

Any combo of seeds goes here—just make sure one is fragrant (try whole fennel, cumin, coriander, or anise seed), and a few are different sizes. Swap larger pumpkin seeds or pine nuts in place of the sunflower seeds, and tiny hemp hearts or flaxseed in place of the sesame.

2 tablespoons sunflower seeds

2 tablespoons sesame seeds

2 tablespoons fennel seeds

1 tablespoon olive oil

¼ teaspoon kosher salt

Combine the sunflower, sesame, and fennel seeds and oil in a small skillet over medium heat. Cook, stirring often, until fragrant and golden, about 2 minutes. Transfer to a bowl and season with the salt. Let cool completely before storing. Seeds will keep in an airtight container in the fridge for up to 1 month.

GARLIC-SHALLOT CRUNCH

Active time: 40 minutes | Total time: 40 minutes | Makes I cup plus ¾ cup tasty oil

In Southeast Asian cooking, crispy fried shallots and garlic add irresistible crunch and a subtle toasted sweetness to everything from curries and noodles to refreshing herb-laden salads. I like them so much and end up wanting them on everything, so making a big batch is the way to go for me. This recipe requires more knife work than any other in the book. I apologize for that, but know that the payoff is worth it. Also, once the shallots and garlic are sliced, the hard part is over. These get crunchier and cook faster if the shallot and garlic are sliced evenly and as thin as possible. If you have a mandoline, use it here. It's not totally necessary, but it makes for easier and faster work. If you're scared of the sharp blade, use a dish towel to hold on to whatever you're slicing or wear a rubber glove (the kind you might wear to wash dishes). Take. Your. Time.

4 large shallots, peeled and thinly sliced into rings (about I cup)

I head garlic, cloves separated and thinly sliced (about ½ cup)

I to I½ cups vegetable or other neutral oil

Kosher salt

Combine the shallots and garlic in a small pot. Add enough vegetable oil just to cover and place over medium heat. When the shallots and garlic are sizzling vigorously, about 4 minutes in, reduce the heat to low. Continue to cook, stirring occasionally, until golden brown, I5 to 20 minutes. Use a slotted spoon to transfer the shallots and garlic to a paper towel–lined plate and season with a little salt. Let oil cool, then store in an airtight container in the fridge for up to I week. Crunchies will keep in an airtight container at room temperature for about I month.

You'll be left with an intensely flavorful oil to boot. Use it to sear fish or make the Sesame-Ginger Dressing on page 62.

CHILI POWDER BLEND

CURRY SPICE BLEND

ZA'ATAR BLEND

SPICE BLENDS

As a professional cook, I have built a pretty wide-ranging spice collection. I've hauled home and been gifted dozens of spices in my day: Spanish pimenton, Japanese togarashi, Moroccan ras el hanout. I include dried chilies here, too. Dare me to resist a bag of shiny red guajillos in an open-air market or from a roadside stand. I cannot.

We all likely have a handful or more of spices in our stash that reflect our culture and our family history, too. (I'm from outside Baltimore City. I bleed Old Bay.)

For the sake of this book, I focus on a core collection of spices, use them often, and combine them in different ways so you use them up while they still sing (ground spices lose their kick after about six months). Some of these spices might be in your pantry already. Some you may have but don't use that often. Some might be brand-new to you.

Spices are a great way to capture the essence of a place and its cuisine. Used in combination with one another, certain spice blends can make a dish recognizable as, say, Indian, Middle Eastern, or Mexican. Those are broad characterizations to be sure. One could spend a lifetime cooking and researching only Oaxacan food or Burmese cuisine, and using a manufactured mix of chili or curry powder is vastly different than harvesting, drying, and cooking with regional ingredients at the elbow of a local. But cooking with these types of blends is a good way to start exploring and expanding culinary horizons beyond your own.

I asked Lior Lev Sercarz—the creator of La Boite, a New York–based spice shop and creator of one-of-a-kind spice blends—about what to look for when shopping for dried spices. He says there's not a whole lot you can know about a spice before you open a jar. It's best to compare brands to find out what you like and can trust. I also spoke with Ethan Frisch, cofounder of Burlap and Barrel, a company that works directly with spice farmers and foragers around the world to maintain traceability (often lost in the process) and unmatched quality. He made the point that spices won't really go bad—mold is rare. What we're working against is staleness. So, buy your spices in small quantities and make your own blends so you use them up more quickly.

There's no one way to make a spice blend: the whole idea is that you can play around with them to suit your own preferences. The blends that follow are approximations of flavors I admire and crave most: a curry powder, a chili powder, and something like za'atar. They're convenient and easy to toss together with spices anyone can find at their closest supermarket and you can customize them to suit your palate. Sometimes I add a little fennel seed to the curry blend or extra cayenne to the chili powder. If I have ground sumac I use it in the za'atar but if not, a little lemon zest adds tang. Plus, unlike premade blends, homemade spice mixes tend to meld and mature over time so they increase in oomph rather than lose it.

SPICE BLENDS

Active time: 5 minutes | **Total time: 5 minutes** | **Makes about ¼ cup**

Add a tablespoon or two to sautéed onions to create a flavorful base for soups or braises (page 247). Combine one with a teaspoon of salt and use it to season a big piece of fish (page 244) or a whole chicken (page 220). Shake some onto shrimp before grilling or fold some into ground lamb for meatballs or kebabs. Add a smattering to buttered boiled potatoes, toss with cucumbers and tomatoes (page 176), or stir into yogurt or mayo for quick dips and spreads.

ZA'ATAR BLEND

Za'atar is an herby, nutty, tangy Middle Eastern spice blend. It's named after its primary ingredient, hyssop leaves, that are dried and blended with toasted sesame seeds, herbs, spices, and ground sumac. Fresh or dried za'atar leaves can be hard to find in American supermarkets but you can use dried oregano or thyme in its place.

I tablespoon ground cumin

I tablespoon ground coriander

I tablespoon sesame seeds

I teaspoon ground sumac or freshly grated lemon zest

I tablespoon dried oregano or thyme

Place ingredients in a jar or other resealable container and shake or stir to combine. Za'atar will keep in an airtight container at room temperature for a couple of months.

CURRY SPICE BLEND

I used to think using a commercial curry powder was frowned upon by Indian home cooks so I made my own, using it in tandem with onions, garlic, and fresh ginger. But cookbook author and photographer Nik Sharma set me straight. "It's a nice idea to make everything from scratch but blends are great shortcuts and there's no stigma around using them." The one warning he offers: many commercial curry powders come with salt or sugar in the mix, so you can lose control of your seasoning. Read labels carefully or try this straightforward combination.

2 tablespoons ground turmeric

2 teaspoons ground cumin

2 teaspoons ground coriander

2 teaspoons ground cinnamon

Place ingredients in a jar or other resealable container and shake or stir to combine. Curry blend will keep in an airtight container at room temperature for a couple of months.

CHILI POWDER BLEND

This Tex-Mex-inspired mix adds earthy depth to soup bases and, of course, chili, and two tablespoons turns a pound of ground meat into the old-school crunchy taco filling of my youth. The dried chili is what makes it "chili powder." Ancho, pasilla, or guajillo chilies are good choices. Toast them in a hot skillet until shiny and beginning to puff. Let cool, remove the seeds if you like, then grind in a spice grinder or high-powered blender. If you don't have dried chilies on hand you can add a little more crushed red pepper or cayenne.

2 dried chilies, toasted, seeded, and ground

2 tablespoons ground cumin

2 tablespoons ground coriander

4 teaspoons dried oregano

¼ to ½ teaspoon crushed red pepper flakes or cayenne pepper

Place ingredients in a jar or other resealable container and shake or stir to combine. Chili Powder will keep in an airtight container at room temperature for a couple of months.

CHILI-LIME-
CUMIN SALT

PEPITA-
BLACK
PEPPER
SALT

LEMON-
SESAME
SALT

A FEW FLAVORED SALTS

When people ask why restaurant food tastes so much better than their own home cooking, the answer is often salt. Not to discount the time and energy restaurant cooks spend sourcing and cooking food for paying customers, but put simply, seasoning early and seasoning often, as you go, is one of the first things they teach you in cooking school. And it can take hours of trial and error to master.

Even when you do, there's an extra-credit seasoning step that a lot of home cooks miss. Recipes often include an instruction to "season to taste" or "taste and adjust seasoning" at the very end. It's a step that's easy to skip. When you're new to cooking, something either tastes good or it doesn't. It's hard to identify what's wrong with a dish, let alone how to fix it. Salt isn't always the answer, but it often is.

I use these three finishing salts to amp up the seasoning for that extra-credit seasoning step. Two of them contain citrus zest for a little brightness and floral aroma; two offer heat from black pepper and crushed red pepper flakes; and two add crunch with the addition of pumpkin or sesame seeds. Examine the dish you are seasoning: is it rich with butter or cheese? Consider using the Chili-Lime-Cumin Salt to help balance those rich flavors. Is the dish already spicy? Try the Lemon-Sesame one for contrast.

A few more ideas: use Chili-Lime-Cumin Salt to rim a margarita or Gingery Citrusade (page 284) glass or finish a citrus salad (page 175). Toss the Lemon-Sesame Salt with freshly popped popcorn, or add a pinch to top Frico-Fried Eggs (page 152). Scatter the Pepita–Black Pepper Salt over the Big Olive Oil Crackers (page 278) before baking, or add a pureed vegetable soup for crunch. Eating sliced raw cucumbers? Use any or all.

CHILI-LIME-CUMIN SALT

Active time: 5 minutes | **Total time: 5 minutes** | **Makes about ⅓ cup**

2 tablespoons cumin seeds

I teaspoon crushed red pepper flakes

I tablespoon finely grated lime zest

2 tablespoons flaky salt

Toast the cumin seeds in a small dry skillet over medium heat, shaking often, until fragrant, I to 2 minutes. Transfer to a bowl and add the crushed red pepper flakes, lime zest, and flaky salt. Stir to combine, rubbing the zest in with your fingers. Leave at room temperature, tossing whenever you think about it, until the zest is dry (a few hours to overnight). Cover and store at room temperature up to 3 months.

PEPITA–BLACK PEPPER SALT

Active time: 5 minutes | **Total time: 5 minutes** | **Makes about ⅓ cup**

¼ cup pumpkin seeds, chopped

I tablespoon coarsely ground black pepper

2 tablespoons flaky salt

Toast the pumpkin seeds in a small dry skillet over medium heat, shaking often, until golden and fragrant, about 2 minutes. Transfer to a bowl and add the black pepper and flaky salt. Stir to combine. Cover and store at room temperature up to 3 months.

LEMON-SESAME SALT

Active time: 5 minutes | **Total time: 5 minutes** | **Makes about ⅓ cup**

¼ cup black or white sesame seeds

I tablespoon finely grated lemon zest

2 tablespoons flaky salt

Toast the sesame seeds in a small dry skillet over medium heat, shaking often, until fragrant, I to 2 minutes. Transfer to a bowl and add the lemon zest and flaky salt. Stir to combine, rubbing the zest in with your fingers. Leave at room temperature, tossing whenever you think about it, until the zest is dry (a few hours to overnight). Cover and store at room temperature up to 3 months.

IN THE FRIDGE
DRESSINGS

When I was growing up, my family ate salad every night. It was nothing fancy: chopped iceberg or romaine, baby spinach as we matured, with carrot ribbons (yes), sliced raw mushrooms or zucchini (no, thank you), and dry dill weed (there's a time and a place). We always had a little repurposed Dijon mustard jar in the fridge filled with "Gigi's dressing," named for my great-grandfather. My mouth still puckers at the memory of a salad bowl filled with crunchy raw vegetables tossed in the bracing mixture of mustard, cider vinegar, and oil.

So I had long been in the habit of making my own dressing when, in the spring of 2019, I participated in a bottled salad dressing taste test for work at *Real Simple*. Over the course of a few days, my coworkers and I tasted roughly 130 dressings, dips, and vinaigrettes to determine the best in a handful of categories. As it goes with a lot of packaged goods, a few brands outshone the rest in every category. The best were zesty and bright or creamy with just a hint of sweetness. The worst were too salty or blindingly acidic; some tasted more like sweetened mayonnaise than real ranch. (If you're going to buy, go for Cindy's Kitchen or Ken's Steakhouse; we loved every variety.)

I liked these. But none were as good as the ones we can make ourselves. Making your own dressings makes salad eating fast and delicious, plus you can use them to sauce simply prepared fish or grilled chicken. It also gives you the freedom to make them how you like, minus fillers, stabilizers, or added sugar. My salad palate was trained on that little jar of Gigi's dressing. I like my vinaigrettes

pretty tart, so I add an extra splash of vinegar or lemon juice. The beauty of making your own means you can adjust the seasoning—vinegar or lemon, herbs or alliums, and salt, always—to suit your preferences and your pantry.

The following dressings are ones I'm psyched to find in the fridge, and I always have the ingredients on hand to shake them up. I'll try to keep two at the ready: something creamy, which doubles as a dip for veggies or chips; and something tangy for everything else, including but not limited to marinating chicken, saucing seared fish or tofu, or tossing with beans and/or tuna for an easy lunch.

I make my dressings in an old peanut butter jar or, in the case of the Dijon one, right in the almost-empty mustard jar, with that hard-to-get spoonful left in the bottom. Just pour in the rest of the ingredients, screw the lid on tight (really tight), and give it a vigorous shake. Do this roughly once a week: I've never known a dressing to go bad, but they will lose their zing.

DIJON VINAIGRETTE

Active time: 10 minutes | Total time: 10 minutes | Makes about 1 cup

This Dijon vinaigrette is almost always in my fridge. It's a little spicy from the mustard, but not too much; a little sweet from the honey, but not too much. Plus, you can make it with a different vinegar each time so you never get bored. And it goes with everything. Toss it with chopped celery and a handful of croutons for a crunchy no-cook side salad. Mix it with cooked beans and hunks of tomato for a summer lunch or bitter greens with oranges and hazelnuts for a light winter one. Spoon it over roasted broccoli or beets and add a handful of toasted nuts. Drizzle on a cold cut sandwich.

1 shallot, finely chopped

1 tablespoon Dijon or whole grain mustard

1 teaspoon honey

½ teaspoon kosher salt

¼ teaspoon freshly ground black pepper

¼ cup red or white wine vinegar, balsamic or sherry vinegar

½ cup olive oil

Combine the shallot, mustard, honey, salt, black pepper, vinegar, and oil in a resealable container (preferably a glass jar with a tight-fitting lid) and shake to combine. Alternatively, whisk together to combine in a large bowl then transfer to a resealable container. Dressing will keep in the fridge for about a week.

GARLICKY LEMON DRESSING

Active time: 10 minutes | Total time: 10 minutes | Makes about ¾ cup

This dressing works on salad, sure, but it's also a great marinade for chicken (see the Spicy Lemon Chicken Salad on page 219), fish, shrimp, or pork, especially when grilled. Lemons can vary wildly in their acidity and size, so be ready to adjust the amount of salt and oil to suit your palate. It should be tangy. Know this: Both salt and fat work to balance acid, so if your dressing tastes really sour, add another pinch of salt. If it's still too tangy, add another tablespoon or two of oil, shake, and taste again. Continue until you get a lip-smacking mmm.

1 garlic clove, grated or finely chopped

Zest (1 teaspoon) and juice (3 to 4 tablespoons) of 1 lemon

1 teaspoon dried oregano or thyme

¾ teaspoon kosher salt

½ cup olive oil

½ teaspoon crushed red pepper flakes, optional

Combine the garlic, zest and lemon juice, oregano, salt, oil, and crushed red pepper, if using, in a resealable container (preferably a glass jar with a tight-fitting lid) and shake to combine. Alternatively, whisk together to combine in a large bowl, then transfer to a resealable container. Dressing will keep in the fridge for about a week.

SESAME-GINGER DRESSING

Active time: 10 minutes | Total time: 10 minutes | Makes about ¾ cup

Toss this one with cold noodles and chopped scallions. Pour over sliced silken tofu or use as a dip for cooked shrimp.

2 tablespoons soy sauce or tamari

2 tablespoons rice vinegar

2 teaspoons grated fresh ginger

1 teaspoon sugar

1 scallion, thinly sliced

1 tablespoon toasted sesame seeds

¼ cup vegetable oil (or garlic-shallot oil from Garlic-Shallot Crunch, page 48)

Combine the soy sauce, vinegar, ginger, sugar, scallion, sesame seeds, and oil in a small jar and shake until well combined. Dressing will keep in the fridge for about a week.

OLIVE & HERB VINAIGRETTE

Active time: 10 minutes | Total time: 10 minutes | Makes about ¾ cup

Almost a salad in itself, this dressing can do a lot of heavy lifting. The olives offer briny flavor and something to chew on, so you can toss them with just one other thing and you're done. This one's also good spooned over sliced fresh mozzarella or tossed with cooled cooked pasta for a quick lunch.

½ cup Castelvetrano or other mild olives, pitted and roughly chopped

¼ cup chopped parsley, cilantro, mint and/or dill

1 celery stalk, finely chopped

3 tablespoons white wine vinegar

¼ cup olive oil

¾ teaspoon kosher salt

Several grinds black pepper

Combine the olives, herbs, celery, vinegar, oil, salt, and black pepper in a small jar and shake until well combined. Vinaigrette will keep in the fridge for about a week.

CREAMY DRESSINGS

Active time: 10 minutes | Total time: 10 minutes | Makes about 1 cup base

I offer you here a blueprint dressing you can use for endless variations. The three that follow are classic combos, but I hope you'll be inspired to put your own spin on them. A few more ideas off the top of my head: stir in a spoonful of pesto or one of the spice blends on page 52; swirl in some Quick Chili Oil (page 70) or blend with a spoonful of Zing! Sauce (page 82). Play around with different combinations and don't feel limited to use them on lettuce alone. Creamy dressings make great dips for crudités or chips, of course, but can work as a sauce for poached shrimp or simple seared fish. A smear can do wonders for a plate of boiled potatoes or (cooked from frozen) french fries.

BASE

½ cup full-fat plain yogurt

¼ cup mayonnaise

2 tablespoons lemon juice

¾ teaspoon kosher salt

A few grinds black pepper

Whisk together the base ingredients. Add one of the following combinations to change it up, then whisk in a little water, a tablespoon at a time, until you've reached your desired consistency. Transfer to a resealable jar or container and refrigerate up to 1 week.

RANCH

Add 2 scallions, thinly sliced; 1 garlic clove, grated, pressed, or finely chopped; and lots of freshly ground black pepper to the base and whisk to combine.

CAESAR

Add 2 anchovy fillets, finely chopped; 1 garlic clove, grated; and ½ cup grated Parmesan to the base and whisk to combine.

CHEESE

Add 4 ounces crumbled feta, goat cheese, or mild blue cheese to the base and whisk to combine.

RED ONION

JALAPEÑO

RAISINS

CUCUMBER

RADISHES

FENNEL

MULBERRIES

IN A PICKLE

I've never met a vegetable I didn't like. I hit the farmer's market with an extra tote, no list, and a fistful of dollar bills, knowing I'll come home with more than enough for a week's worth of meals. I think this is ultimately a good quality. Spontaneity! Variety! Vegetables! The only downside is that there are always a couple of things in my crisper that have seen better days: wrinkly beets, floppy celery, fennel with the frilly tops gone brown. What do I do? Pickle them! How do I do it? Vinegar! Plus a few other pantry ingredients.

A punchy brine of vinegar, salt, and spices gives even sad vegetables a pick-me-up. It also lengthens their shelf life for weeks—sometimes months. Preserving minimizes the guilt of buying in excess, and you can use the results in dozens of ways. It works with underripe stone fruit like plums and peaches, too. Those are especially good paired with pork. Even dried fruit works. Pickled raisins cut the richness of pan-fried cutlets or braised chicken thighs, and are delicious with a crispy-skinned roast chicken. Pickled chilies complete the nachos. Cucumbers stand alone.

I pickle quickly; that is, I don't worry about sterilizing jars and store everything in the fridge straightaway. These "quickles" will be ready to enjoy as soon as they're cool, but their flavor will change and develop the longer they sit in the brine. I once complained to a chef friend that some pickled radishes I made were *too* funky. "Just let 'em sit," she advised. Sure enough, after a few more days the funk had mellowed and they made a tasty addition to that night's grain bowl.

If you want to pickle just one thing, start with red onions. They can transform simple egg tacos, defrosted chili, even plain chopped romaine into a lip-smacking meal. But they're very good alongside more onions, particularly roasted ones. As a plus, they turn a gorgeous magenta.

Quickles make appearances throughout this book in salads, with sausages, or on top of curried chickpeas. Once you have them around, you'll come up with even more ways to use them.

QUICKLES

Active time: 15 minutes | Total time: 15 minutes (plus cooling) | Makes 1 pint

FOR THE VEGETABLES

Choose any one of the following (the quantity of which doesn't matter that much, just chop or slice enough to comfortably fit in your jar with a little bit of room at the top):

4 to 6 celery stalks, cut to fit the size of your jar

1 English cucumber or 3 Persian cucumbers, thinly sliced or cut into spears that fit your jar

1 red onion, beet, or fennel bulb, thinly sliced

1 bunch radishes, thinly sliced

4 to 6 fresh chilies, sliced

1½ cups raisins or other dried fruit

FOR THE BRINE

1 cup cider, white wine, or rice vinegar

1 tablespoon kosher salt

1 tablespoon mustard, coriander, or cumin seeds

1 tablespoon sugar

½ teaspoon crushed red pepper flakes, optional

Freshly ground black pepper

Place the vegetables, chilies, or dried fruit in a large resealable container (preferably glass). Combine the vinegar, salt, seeds, sugar, crushed red pepper flakes, if using, and several grinds of black pepper in a small saucepan and bring to a simmer. Give the pan a swirl or two to help the sugar and salt dissolve, then pour the mixture over the vegetables. Add water to cover and let cool to room temperature. Cover tightly and refrigerate up to a month.

You can mix your vegetables when you pickle them if you like. Just remember that if you add chilies everything will be spicy; if you add a beet everything will be red, etc.

HOT STUFF

I really like spicy food. Some former coworkers used to tease me when we were tasting recipes during development. I was always saying, "Does this need heat?"

"Dawn," they'd say. "They're cinnamon rolls."

To each their own!

Next to salt, heat is my favorite way to season a dish. I keep a variety of spicy condiments around—hot sauces, spicy pastes, chili crunches, and the like. When I began to write recipes for this book, I pulled all of the hots from the fridge and pantry. I was a little embarrassed to count fourteen different options, including Sambal Oelek, lime leaf sambal, two types of harissa, a small tin of Thai green curry paste, chili crisp, two types of Sichuan chili oil, a jar of oil packed Calabrian chilies, some belachan sauce a friend brought back from Singapore, a bottle of homemade chili oil made by another friend in Brooklyn, spicy pickled peppers, spicy Spanish peppers. And I'm out of Cholula. Please note that this tally does not include spices like crushed red pepper flakes, dried chilies, and so on.

What I like about these condiments is that they each offer something unique: a little numbing from Sichuan peppercorns in that chili oil, a bit of funk from dried shrimp in Sambal Oelek, floral notes from the Calabrian chilies, a kick of vinegar on the finish in the pepperoncini. But that's also why I like to make my own.

I keep it simple: oil, crushed red pepper flakes, garlic, and a pinch of cinnamon for warmth. The finished oil is hot but versatile enough to be used morning, noon, and night. Try a little over yogurt and cucumbers or eggs. A spoonful revives leftover grains and wakes up soups so it warms you up from the inside out. Drizzle it over pizza, simply steamed broccoli, or pasta with Parmesan cheese.

Infusing oil with chilies (and other dried spices for that matter) is a great way to add big flavor on the fly. In Indian cooking this technique—and the resulting oil—is called *tadka* (though it goes by other names depending on the region). It's a method used to bloom or temper dried spices or other flavorings in hot fat and can be used to finish and flavor a dish, like a simple pot of dal or raita.

Adding a drizzle of chili oil is a good way to adjust heat for various palates, too, just before you serve a dish. I love spicy stuff. The kids? Not yet. Rather than watch them paw at their tongues, I serve the younger set a gently seasoned portion, then ramp up the flavor for game grown-ups.

The following recipe is a jumping-off point. You can add other dried spices or flavorings to the base—a tablespoon of chopped ginger, a strip of orange zest, maybe a teaspoon of whole cumin seeds—and see what works for you. What you're sure to like is turning store-bought pantry ingredients into something bigger and bolder than their parts.

QUICK CHILI OIL

Active time: 10 minutes | Total time: 10 minutes (plus cooling) | Makes about ½ cup

½ cup vegetable or other neutral oil

1 tablespoon crushed red pepper flakes

2 garlic cloves, grated or finely chopped

Pinch cinnamon

Combine the oil, pepper flakes, garlic, and cinnamon in a small pot and set over low heat. Cook, stirring or swirling occasionally, until the oil is bright orange and fragrant, about 8 minutes. Let cool, transfer to a resealable jar, and refrigerate up to 1 month.

SOME MORE IDEAS FOR CHILI OIL:

- Swirl into Greek yogurt with a few chopped scallions for a quick dip for chips
- Drizzle over a steak salad
- Pool atop hummus or white bean dip
- Mix with a tablespoon each soy sauce and rice vinegar as a dip for frozen (or homemade) dumplings
- Spoon over brothy soups or Office Bowls (page 264)
- Drip over deviled eggs
- Add to a split biscuit topped with butter and runny honey
- Stir into guacamole
- Smear a little (or a lot) on a toasted bagel with cream cheese
- Fry an egg in it. Good morning!

COOKED VEGETABLES

I once interviewed a seasoned food and recipe writer who complained about showing up to a catered event where there were both "roasted root vegetables" and "roasted beets" on the buffet. "Um, *hello*," he said. "Those are the same thing."

I pointed out that he'd been extolling the ease and versatility of roasting big batches of vegetables for the previous decade. "Do you think that's maybe your fault?" I asked. He laughed, thank heaven.

Roasting is perhaps the easiest way to make a large amount of vegetables not only edible but delicious—caramelized and tender—all in one shot. Plus my kids really like them. Knock wood.

I roast at least two baking sheets' worth of vegetables every week. Sometimes more than that. They're great tasting that day and make for nice leftovers, too, whether chopped and tossed into stir-fried grains, or tucked inside a taco.

But roasted vegetables aren't the only cooked veg I keep around. Almost every week I boil some small potatoes and cook a few bunches of dark leafy greens. The potatoes get smashed or crushed and tossed with flavored oil or quickly caramelized onions. I toss the greens into pasta or tuck them into pies.

Having precooked vegetables around has made a huge impact on how well my family and I eat throughout the week. And by "well," I just mean that we eat a lot more vegetables. And isn't that the idea?

HOW TO ROAST VEGETABLES

Some good vegetables for roasting: sweet potatoes, cauliflower, broccoli, carrots, beets, radishes, cabbage, onions, eggplant, winter squash, summer squash, and kohlrabi. Basically, you can roast almost anything firm. Sliced or chopped is fine, thin or thick is OK; just make sure that the pieces are roughly the same size and/or thickness. But don't fret over this too much, either. Some extra crispy bits and some just-tender spots are what made a sheet of roasted vegetables extra delicious.

Preheat the oven to 425°F. Arrange **chopped vegetables** on a rimmed baking sheet in a single layer so they're not overlapping. Grab a second baking sheet if you think things might be too crowded. Toss the chopped vegetables with **olive oil**. I find about 3 tablespoons is enough for a single sheet. Depending on the moisture content of whatever you're roasting, you might need a little more, but probably not less. Toss the vegetables with your hands. They (the vegetables and your hands) should be evenly coated with oil. Season everything with **kosher salt**, about ½ teaspoon per baking sheet to start, and several grinds of black pepper. Grab the side of the sheet and give it a shake. I find this move seasons everything pretty evenly and gives you a sense if things really are too crowded. Items should have room to scoot around a little bit.

If you're roasting one sheet, put it on the middle rack. If you're roasting two sheets, put them on racks in the upper and lower third positions. Roast, shaking the sheets at the halfway mark with that same move you used to season initially. The fastest roasting vegetables will be done in 20 to 25 minutes (sweet potatoes go pretty quickly), but every vegetable is different. Set your timer for 20 minutes and start checking. You're looking for tender and *deeply* browned in spots. Serve immediately or let cool and store in an airtight container in the fridge for about a week. Or freeze for as long as your freezer can be trusted.

HOW TO BOIL POTATOES

Put **some potatoes** (tiny gold potatoes are my favorite) in an appropriate-size pot. (Quarter any very big potatoes first, otherwise I just throw them in whole.) Cover the potatoes with **cold water** by about an inch. Add **2 tablespoons kosher salt** and place over medium-high heat. Bring to a boil, reduce the heat slightly if it's really rocking and rolling in there, and cook until a knife or fork inserted in the potatoes slides in easily. Drain and return to the pot to cool and dry. Potatoes can be refrigerated in an airtight container for about a week. See page 192 for some easy ways to use them.

HOW TO LONG-COOK GREENS

The following method works the same for four bunches of greens as it does for two

or three, making it a great way to keep whatever greens you do have ready to eat. Once you cook the greens, eat them hot or cold on their own as a side dish, add them to rice or grain bowls, chop and add to sautéed beans—I like cannellini, gigante, or black-eyed peas—and pile on toast, or fold them into pasta. Or a frittata. Or an omelet. Or scrambled eggs. Got it? They freeze well, too; defrost overnight in the fridge. Here's how to make them:

Bring a large pot of water to a boil and season with a good handful of **kosher salt**.

Add **hearty greens** such as kale, collards, mustard greens, or chard, trimmed and cut crosswise into 2-inch strips (don't fuss over this, just give a rough chop through the stems) and stir to wilt, about 20 seconds. Using a slotted spoon or tongs, transfer to a colander to drain.

Heat enough **olive oil** to cover the bottom of a large, heavy-bottomed pot over medium-high heat. Add a few smashed and peeled **garlic cloves** and a pinch or two **crushed red pepper flakes** (or 1 crushed chili de arbol), if you want these spicy. Cook, stirring often, until fragrant and garlic is golden, a minute or two.

Add the drained greens, season with **kosher salt** and **freshly ground black pepper**, and stir to coat in the oil. Cover the pot, reduce heat to low, and cook, uncovering to stir a few times, until very tender, about 20 minutes. Uncover the pot and continue to cook, stirring occasionally, until any liquid in the bottom of the pot evaporates, 2 to 5 minutes. Eat right away or wait. Greens will keep for about a week in the fridge or frozen up to 1 month.

SAUCES AND PASTES

These recipes are not for sauces in the traditional sense. They are not made in a skillet after browning meat. There are no brunoised vegetables, no deglazed pans. There is no mounting of butter involved. That's how you learn to "build a sauce" in culinary school.

The old way with sauces is, in my opinion, fussy and stressful and in most cases decidedly French. Not that there's anything wrong with classic French cuisine, but we are lucky to live in a time when we have access to cooks and flavors from around the world.

I use the words "sauces" and "pastes" loosely to describe the following pourable and/or spreadable homemade staples. A few are inspired by my days as a twenty-something living in San Francisco where I was experiencing some of these flavors for the very first time. They were blowing my mind. The Zing! Sauce (page 82) is a love letter to my favorite burrito at Taqueria Cancún on Mission Street. I'd split the vegetarian option (pinto beans, no rice, extra verde). "It's good to share," my coworker Nicole said.

The Out-of-Season Salsa, too (page 82), conjures memories of the paper-lined plastic baskets of free chips and salsa at Taqueria Cancún. The Tahini Sauce (page 80) takes me around the corner to Truly Mediterranean on Sixteenth Street, where I had my first falafel sandwich.

The other recipes lean hard into flavors I grew up on: slow roasting tomatoes to approximate the jammy intensity of a sun-dried tomato; lacing Hellmann's (or your favorite) mayonnaise with garlic and lemon juice; or lazily mixing all of the conventional ballpark offerings to create a condiment all your own.

Use the recipes in this section to add flavor and moisture wherever you need it: on grain bowls, tacos, or crispy pitas; on a patty melt, over eggs, or inside a grilled cheese.

SLOW-ROASTED
TOMATOES

SPICY
TURMERIC
TAHINI

CILANTRO-
LIME TAHINI

INSTANT
AIOLI

OUT-OF-
SEASON
SALSA

SLOW-ROASTED TOMATOES

Active time: 10 minutes | Total time: 2 hours | Makes about 2 cups

The best tomatoes are grown between July and September. Grown in your own backyard, a neighbor's, or picked up at the farmers market, a ripe summer tomato can be truly sublime. But slow-roasting tomatoes is a fantastic way to improve subpar tomatoes any time of year. Cooking them low and slow concentrates their sweetness, what so many out-of-season options are missing.

Use this recipe to upgrade lackluster tomatoes, adjusting the time as necessary if they're very large. Toss the flavorful finished product with pasta, top a BLT, or add to the pita chips salad on page 176. Fold them into scrambled eggs or spoon over sliced fresh mozzarella for caprese vibes.

4 pints tomatoes (about 3 pounds), halved

¼ cup olive oil

1 teaspoon kosher salt

Freshly ground black pepper

A few sprigs fresh thyme or oregano or ½ teaspoon dried thyme or oregano, optional

Preheat the oven to 300°F. On a rimmed baking sheet, toss the tomatoes with the oil, salt, several grinds of black pepper, and the thyme, if using. Arrange the tomatoes cut-side up and roast until slightly shrunken but not dry, about 1 hour for cherry or grape tomatoes and up to 90 minutes for slightly bigger ones. Refrigerate in an airtight container for up to 1 week.

TAHINI SAUCE

Active time: 5 minutes | Total time: 5 minutes | Makes about ½ cup base

What's cool about this sauce is that you can make it thick, like a dip or spread—great for pita or smearing under grilled vegetables—or thin it out with a little water and use it as a dressing or for a salad or Office Bowls (page 264). Tahini can seize when you add other liquids to it. Don't get nervous if that happens. Just add more water, a little at a time, until you've reached your desired consistency. Abide by the manufacturer's instructions for storage. Some suggest refrigeration after opening, but this can hamper spreadability. Still, I keep mine in the fridge and stir it with a fork to get things moving again.

¼ cup tahini

2 tablespoons lemon juice

2 tablespoons olive oil

¼ teaspoon kosher salt

Freshly ground black pepper

¼ cup water (or more), optional

> Use a blender here for a smoother sauce.

Whisk together the tahini, lemon juice, oil, salt, a few grinds of black pepper, and the water in a medium bowl until smooth. Store in an airtight container in the refrigerator for up to 3 weeks.

To change it up, stir one of the following combinations into the base:

SPICY TURMERIC
½ teaspoon ground turmeric
¼ teaspoon cayenne pepper or crushed red pepper flakes

HONEY-MISO
2 tablespoons white or yellow miso paste
I teaspoon honey

CILANTRO-LIME
½ bunch fresh cilantro (about I cup roughly chopped leaves and tender stems)
2 tablespoons lime juice

GARLIC-YOGURT
¼ cup plain yogurt
I garlic clove, pressed or grated

ZING! SAUCE

Active time: 5 minutes | Total time: 5 minutes | Makes about ½ cup

Herby green sauces like chimichurri, chermoula, zhug and salsa verde are some of my favorite condiments. They add instant salt, tang, spice and freshness wherever you add them. Though this one started as a way to stretch a bunch of wilting cilantro, the bright, spicy sauce gets used in my house more than any other in this section. I encourage you to try it on, well, everything: grilled chicken or steamed clams, roasted broccoli, eggs, a hot dog. You can swirl it into yogurt for a quick veggie dip or stir it into mayonnaise and spread on a sandwich.

I cup chopped fresh herbs, such as parsley, cilantro, basil, mint, or a combination

I jalapeño or serrano chili, seeded for less heat, roughly chopped

I garlic clove, smashed

¼ cup vegetable or olive oil

2 tablespoons lime juice

¾ teaspoon kosher salt

Combine the herbs, jalapeño, garlic, oil, lime juice, and salt in a blender or food processor and process until smooth. Sauce will keep in the fridge for about a week. Give it a stir before using.

OUT-OF-SEASON SALSA

Active time: 5 minutes | Total time: 5 minutes | Makes about 2½ cups

For salsa emergencies: Dump. Blend. Dip. It doesn't get easier than this. I make this blender salsa throughout the year with canned tomatoes, but you can make it with fresh tomatoes if you have them.

One 14-ounce can whole peeled tomatoes (cherry tomatoes if you can find them)

2 garlic cloves, smashed and peeled

½ bunch cilantro, roughly chopped (about I cup)

½ red or white onion, roughly chopped

Juice of 2 limes (3 to 4 tablespoons)

I jalapeño or serrano chili, seeded for less heat, roughly chopped

1½ teaspoons kosher salt

½ teaspoon ground cumin

Combine the whole peeled tomatoes and their juice, the garlic, cilantro, onion, lime juice, jalapeño, salt and cumin in a blender or food processor and pulse to desired consistency. Refrigerate in an airtight container for up to I week.

HOUSE SAUCE

Active time: 5 minutes | Total time: 5 minutes | Makes about ½ cup

You don't have to make this ahead, but I put it in this fridge section because of the spirit of the thing. The ingredients are there, waiting. You don't really need to measure, either: just two squeezes to one squeeze to one squeeze plus a dash if you like. And, as always, play around with it. No ketchup? Try it without. French's only? Also worth a try. I tend to make this one right before I'm going to use it because it's so fast and easy, but if you love it, make a double batch and keep it around for a week or so. Use it on burgers or sausages, for dipping french fries or boiled or roasted potatoes, or as the secret sauce in a patty melt or turkey sandwich.

¼ cup mayonnaise

2 tablespoons ketchup

2 tablespoons Dijon mustard

1 teaspoon hot sauce (Sriracha, Sambal, Tabasco, or your preferred), optional

Freshly ground black pepper

Mix the mayonnaise, ketchup, mustard, hot sauce, if using, and several grinds of black pepper together in a small bowl. Refrigerate in an airtight container until ready to use, up to a week.

INSTANT AIOLI

Active time: 5 minutes | Total time: 5 minutes | Makes about ½ cup

This is just garlicky lemon mayo, but I'm always surprised by how dramatically it upgrades the things I serve it with. Fold it into crushed boiled potatoes, or serve it with crispy buttered potatoes or Tater Tots. Use it as a dip for cold cooked shrimp—they're in the freezer, right?—or spread a spoonful under a crispy chicken cutlet. It works on a BLT or a burger or wherever you spread mayonnaise in the first place.

½ cup mayonnaise

1 garlic clove, grated

1 tablespoon lemon juice, plus more

½ teaspoon kosher salt

Freshly ground black pepper

Mix the mayonnaise, garlic, lemon juice, salt, and a few grinds of black pepper in a small bowl until smooth, adding more lemon juice if you like. Any extra will keep in an airtight container in the refrigerator up to 2 days.

CARAMEL
SAUCE

CHOCOLATE
SAUCE

FROZEN
FRUIT JAM

DRIVE-THRU SAUCES

This triad of sauces was developed with a certain fast food sundae in mind. You remember the options: chocolate, caramel, or strawberry sauces over creamy vanilla soft serve, topped with crunchy salted peanuts. Caramel was my favorite. I remember eating carefully in the front seat of the car, the window down, sliding my spoon down the side of the plastic cup in an attempt to retrieve a perfectly balanced bite of sauce, ice cream, and nuts.

I don't expect you to make hot fudge or caramel sauce *or* jam on the regular. But they are really easy to whip up with what you likely already have. And when you need an ice cream sundae, you can.

Try any of these sweet sauces drizzled over pancakes (wow) or smeared on thick slices of toast. Promise me you'll try them layered with slightly softened vanilla ice cream or lightly sweetened whipped cream, and don't forget the peanuts.

CARAMEL SAUCE

Active time: 15 minutes | Total time: 15 minutes (plus cooling) | Makes about 1½ cups

Caramel is one of my favorite things to make. I love to watch the sugar slowly dissolve and turn amber. I love the drama as it bubbles up, seizes, then softens to a silky nappé (that is, thick enough to coat the back of a spoon). This one's made with whole milk because I always have it. Heavy cream yields a slightly more luscious sauce, but you can use just about any liquid in the milk's place. Try water for a leaner sauce, red wine, or even cooled coffee. I insist you drizzle it over the Chocolate Skillet Cake (page 289).

1 cup sugar

2 tablespoons water

4 tablespoons unsalted butter, cut into four pieces

½ cup milk or heavy cream

½ teaspoon pure vanilla extract

½ teaspoon kosher salt

Combine the sugar and water in a medium pot and stir until evenly moistened. Set the pot over medium heat and cook, undisturbed, until the sugar melts and the mixture begins to turn amber (it will turn first in a little spot that then grows), 10 to 12 minutes. Gently swirl the pan until everything is evenly amber in color. Add the butter and swirl until melted. Remove from the heat and whisk in the milk until smooth and combined. Add the vanilla and salt and stir to combine. Let cool slightly before serving. Refrigerate in an airtight container for up to 1 month.

FROZEN FRUIT JAM

Active time: 20 minutes | Total time: 25 minutes (plus cooling) | Makes about 1 cup

Once in a while I find myself simmering a batch of jam with whatever frozen fruit I have on hand. This recipe is a straightforward formula that works for most frozen (or fresh) fruit, but mixed berries and pineapple are my favorite variations. Play around with different combinations of fruit and citrus, or try it without the vanilla to see what you prefer. Use the finished fruit spread in the Sparkly Jam and Nut Tart (page 307), or dolloped on a Dutch Baby with Jam (page 137). Or, duh, with peanut butter.

1 pound frozen berries, chopped frozen pineapple, or chopped frozen peaches

1 cup sugar

Pinch kosher salt

Juice of 1 lemon or lime

1 teaspoon pure vanilla extract, optional

Combine the berries, sugar, salt, lemon juice, vanilla, if using, and ¼ cup water in a medium saucepan. Bring to a simmer and cook, stirring and mashing occasionally, until thickened and the bubbles slow (it will continue to thicken as it cools), 18 to 20 minutes. Let cool, then transfer to a jar or other resealable glass container. Jam will keep in the fridge for about a month or in the freezer for 3 months.

CHOCOLATE SAUCE

Active time: 10 minutes | Total time: 10 minutes | Makes about 1½ cups

The chocolate sauce can be made with whatever semi- or bittersweet chocolate you have around, even a bag of classic semisweet morsels. It's pourable when warm and spreadable once chilled—excellent for sandwiching between Ritz crackers or eating straight from a spoon.

6 ounces (1 cup) semi- or bittersweet chocolate chips or chopped chocolate

¾ cup heavy cream

¼ cup brown sugar

¼ teaspoon kosher salt

½ teaspoon pure vanilla extract

Vanilla extract rounds out the sauce but a splash of whiskey or other liqueur is a nice adults-only substitution.

Place the chocolate in a medium bowl. Combine the cream, brown sugar, and salt in a small pot and set over medium heat. Cook, stirring often, until the sugar is dissolved and the cream is about to simmer, about 5 minutes. Pour the cream mixture over the chocolate and let sit for 1 minute. Add the vanilla and whisk until the chocolate melts and the mixture is smooth. Let cool slightly before serving. Refrigerate in an airtight container for up to 3 weeks. Reheat in 10-second intervals in the microwave until pourable.

IN THE FREEZER
A TOMATO
DUO

I am never without tomato sauce. I toss it with pasta (page 227), spoon it over crispy chicken cutlets (page 224), and use it on homemade pizza bagels. And while I always have a backup jar of marinara in the pantry, I still prefer to make my own. It's fast and easy, and I know exactly what's in it (so many jarred sauces are loaded with sugar and too sweet for my taste). These two sauces are my go-tos. One fast and lean, one meaty and rich, they cover all the bases.

A quick note on canned tomatoes (also see page 8): I have spent the better part of the last decade singing the praises of canned whole peeled tomatoes, convinced that only the best were preserved in their entirety (minus the skins, of course). But Mindy Fox, a food friend, cookbook author, and Italian food expert, recently told me crushed tomatoes were her preference, as they're more tomatoey in flavor. I trust Mindy implicitly, so I gave them a try. And wouldn't you know it, she was right.

Crushed tomatoes can boost the flavor in the quick 15-Minute Marinara (page 90). If you have kids or, ahem, a grown-up who doesn't like any texture, feel free to throw the finished sauce into the blender to get it smooth. That'll only take another minute.

Use whatever canned tomatoes you have on hand for the 53-Minute Ragu (page 91). Because it's fortified with butter and sausage it's delicious any way you simmer it. I was originally going for a one-hour sauce, but when I made it, I got to the fifty-three-minute mark and had to leave to pick up my kids from daycare. Point being, it's flexible. It's good at both fifty-three minutes and one hour; if you have to do something else, don't fret over the sauce. It'll wait.

For either, I use about 1½ to 2 cups of sauce per pound of pasta, then freeze the rest in pint-size containers so it's ready for the next round. But these sauces go with more than pasta: add them to a bowl of creamy polenta or grits, spread on a split baguette and top with a melty cheese, or use in place of tomatoes in the Pizza Broccoli on page 207.

15-MINUTE MARINARA

Active time: 15 minutes | Total time: 15 minutes | Makes 2 quarts

½ cup oil

2 yellow onions, chopped

2 garlic cloves, finely chopped

2½ teaspoons kosher salt, divided

Freshly ground black pepper

Two 28-ounce cans tomatoes (crushed preferred, or whole peeled)

A little bit of water to rinse out the can (about ¾ cup but I don't expect you to measure this)

Heat the oil in a medium pot over medium-high heat. Add the onions, garlic, 1 teaspoon salt, and several grinds of black pepper. Cook, stirring often, until the onions are translucent, about 5 minutes. Add the tomatoes and water, the remaining 1½ teaspoons salt, and some more black pepper.

Bring to a simmer and cook, stirring occasionally, until slightly reduced, about 10 minutes. Blend if you like. Let cool, then divide the sauce into pint-size containers. Refrigerate for about a week or freeze up to 6 months.

Makes the equivalent of two 32-ounce jars.

53-MINUTE RAGU

Active time: 15 minutes | Total time: About an hour | Makes about 5 cups

I stick unsalted butter

I large yellow onion, chopped

4 garlic cloves, finely chopped, grated, or pressed

I pound sweet Italian sausage, casings removed, ground beef, or ground pork

2 teaspoons kosher salt, divided

Freshly ground black pepper

2 tablespoons tomato paste

Few sprigs fresh oregano or I teaspoon dried oregano

½ teaspoon crushed red pepper flakes, optional

½ cup red or white wine, optional

One 28-ounce can crushed or whole peeled tomatoes

Parmesan rind, optional

Melt the butter in a large, heavy-bottom pot or Dutch oven over medium high heat. Add the onion and garlic and cook, stirring often, until translucent, 3 to 5 minutes. Add the sausage and I teaspoon of salt. Cook, stirring and breaking up the sausage with a spoon or spatula, until it starts to turn golden and the bottom of the pot starts to brown, too, 8 to 10 minutes. Add the tomato paste, oregano, and crushed red pepper flakes, if using, and cook, stirring, until the tomato paste is slightly darker in color, I to 2 minutes. Add the wine, if using, bring to a simmer, and cook for I minute.

Add the crushed tomatoes. If using whole peeled tomatoes, place them in a small bowl, along with their juices, and crush them with your hands, then add them to the pot. Rinse out the can with about ¾ cup of water and add that liquid to the pot along with the remaining I teaspoon salt and the Parmesan rind, if using. Bring to a simmer, stirring occasionally. Reduce the heat to medium-low and cook, partially covered, until slightly reduced, 20 to 30 minutes. Let cool, then transfer the sauce to pint-size containers. Refrigerate for about a week or freeze up to 6 months.

GOLDEN
CHICKEN STOCK

Active time: 10 minutes | Total time: 2 hours | Makes 12 cups

I am happy to buy chicken broth or stock. It's fast, it's convenient. But I refuse to waste a perfectly good chicken carcass. So I make chicken stock every time I roast a bird. And you should, too. Use the leftover bones from the Slow Roasted Chicken on page 220 to make this easy stock, or start with any roast chicken recipe you like. Use the finished liquid gold in soups or braises, or sip it out of a big mug.

1 chicken carcass, or a rough equivalent of leftover chicken parts

2 yellow onions, unpeeled, halved

2 carrots, broken in half

2 celery stalks, broken in half

2 bay leaves

1 head garlic, halved crosswise

1 tablespoon black peppercorns

Two big pinches kosher salt

Put the chicken, onions, carrots, celery, bay leaves, garlic, peppercorns, and salt into the biggest pot you have and cover with cold water by about an inch. Bring to a simmer over medium heat (watch carefully so it doesn't boil over) and cook, partially covered, until the stock is golden and slightly reduced, about 90 minutes. Let cool slightly.

Using tongs or a slotted spoon, discard any big pieces of vegetables and bones. Set a colander inside a large bowl. Pour the stock into the colander to catch any of the remaining smaller pieces. (If you have a large fine-mesh sieve, great! Use it. I don't have one, but it will make for a clearer stock.) Let cool, then transfer the strained stock to pint- or quart-size containers. Refrigerate up to 5 days or freeze up to 6 months.

MEATBALLS

I was obsessed with perfecting meatballs as a young cook. I modified meat mixtures, adjusted my ratios of protein to egg to bread crumbs to cheese. I tweaked and tinkered, taking my time over a hot skillet, browning and turning, certain that pan-frying was essential to their deliciousness.

At the time, my friend Kari asked me to teach her how to make meatballs. When we got to the searing part, the meatballs spattered hot fat as they crisped. Kari jumped back. "How do you do this without getting burned?" she yelped. I think I said something like, "You get used to it." This was the price, I believed, of perfection.

Cut to me making meatballs now and I'm tired of getting splashed with hot fat. I've converted. Now I only cook meatballs in the oven. It's easier, faster, and no less delicious. And you don't have to clean the whole stovetop when you're done. And nobody gets hurt! Kari, please accept these Neatballs as my humble apology.

My favorite meatballs are made with 80/20 ground chuck (that's beef). That 20 percent fat keeps the meatballs nice and juicy so you don't have to add a bunch of other stuff to keep them moist. Ground pork is my second favorite, followed by meat loaf mix—usually a combination of ground beef, pork, and veal. Ground turkey, preferably dark meat, works, too, but turkey breast is also fine. The only protein I'd caution you against is ground chicken, which is a little too wet and soft. However, if ground chicken is what you have, or what you prefer, go for it (though you may need to add another quarter cup of bread crumbs to help the chickenballs hold their shape).

This one adaptable recipe yields an entire batch of meatballs ready for simmering, saucing, or sandwiching in just about twelve minutes. Once baked, drop them into brothy soups or transfer to a pot of bubbling marinara (page 90); toss with your favorite pasta shape or serve over creamy polenta. Smash on top of toasted crusty bread or a split English muffin, cover with cheese, and broil. Serve over rice with a spoonful of Zing! Sauce (page 82). Or line them up in a toasted, mayo-slathered hoagie roll or hot dog bun, top with pickled onions (page 66) or jalapeños, smoosh, halve, and serve.

This meatball recipe doubles super easily, so bake a double (or triple!) batch, let them cool, and freeze as many as you want. When you're ready to reheat, toss them onto a baking sheet at 350°F until warmed through, about fifteen minutes. Proceed however you like.

95

OVEN-BAKED NEATBALLS

Active time: 10 minutes | Total time: 25 minutes | Makes about 24 meatballs

½ cup whole milk

½ cup panko, crushed crackers, or Oil and Herb Croutons (page 46), crushed

½ cup grated Parmesan or pecorino

1 large egg

1½ teaspoons kosher salt

1 garlic clove, grated

1 teaspoon fennel seeds, chopped

1 teaspoon dried oregano

Freshly ground black pepper

1 pound ground beef, pork, meatloaf mix, or turkey

Preheat the oven to 425°F.

Mix the milk, panko, Parmesan, egg, salt, garlic, fennel seeds, oregano, and several grinds of black pepper in a large bowl. Add the meat and, using clean hands, fold everything together until evenly combined. Roll the mixture into 1½-inch balls and place on an ungreased rimmed baking sheet.

Bake until sizzling and no longer pink, about 10 minutes. Increase the heat to broil and broil until lightly browned on top, about 3 more minutes.

To freeze: let cool completely, then transfer to a resealable plastic bag. Freeze up to 6 months.

FREEZER PESTO

I never thought I would be the type of mom who hid vegetables in my kids' food. Since I love vegetables, I thought, they will too. They'll be able to identify their kale from their collards and name-check carrots by the farmers who grew them. Then I had kids. And the realities of feeding someone who is only medium curious about vegetables and hardly able to sit still for five minutes set in.

I do all the things experts encourage you to do when introducing new foods: I present the vegetables—up to twenty times, they say!—each time hopeful that on this occasion my daughter will take to the peas, the non-french-fried potato, the dark greens. By some miracle she loves a "market salad" (it's all in the branding), but when it comes to other greens, we can't quite get past romaine.

So I turn to pesto, by which I mean "green puree with cheese." It's a great way to incorporate greens into a diet that is largely composed of buttered fusilli and quesadillas. It's also an efficient repository for any greens or tender herbs on the verge of a nervous wilt. As long as the greens—steamed asparagus, roasted broccoli, blanched kale—are tender enough to blend or food-process, they can be used in pesto. It even works with a frozen (thawed and squeezed) brick of spinach.

Once processed, pesto will keep in the fridge for about a week, but I like to freeze the mixture in a silicone ice cube tray in one-ounce portions. Once firm, pop the cubes out into a resealable plastic bag and store them in the freezer for up to three months. Two cubes is the perfect amount of sauce for eight ounces of pasta. It's a terrific way to disguise

a serving of spinach as cheesy green spaghetti, but other award-winning applications include:

- **Green Rice** (or other grains): Cook rice according to package directions. Remove from heat, add 1 cube pesto for each cup of rice, and let steam, covered, 5 minutes. Toss to combine.

- **Sandwich Schmear:** Thaw a cube and spread a couple of spoonfuls of pesto on a sandwich (turkey, pesto, Swiss, and red onion is a divine combination), or try it inside a grilled cheese (page 215).

- **Au Pistou:** Add a cube to mostly vegetable soups, brothy beans, or steamed clams (page 239). Not only does the pesto add great color and flavor, but it cools the soup to perfect slurping temperature.

- **Green Dressing:** Thaw a cube and shake into a simple vinaigrette.

- **Dip:** Thaw and swirl into yogurt as an easy dip for chips or crudité.

- **Shake-n-Bake:** Thaw a cube and slather onto chicken breasts or thighs. Scatter with bread crumbs and bake until crumbs are golden and chicken is cooked through.

- **Green Eggs:** Thaw a cube and stir a spoonful into scrambled eggs.

FLEXO-PESTO

Active time: 10 minutes | Total time: 10 minutes | Makes about 1½ cups

6 cups greens such as spinach, kale, arugula, and/or tender herbs such as basil or parsley or a combination (5 ounces)

1 garlic clove

½ cup toasted nuts or seeds such as almonds, pine nuts, walnuts, hazelnuts, pecans, pistachios, pepitas, sunflower seeds, or a combination

½ cup olive oil

¾ teaspoon kosher salt

Freshly ground black pepper

2 ounces (½ cup) grated Parmesan or pecorino, optional

Combine the greens and/or herbs, garlic, and nuts in a food processor and pulse until finely chopped, stopping the machine and scraping down the sides of the bowl as needed.

With the machine running, stream in the olive oil. Stop the machine, scrape down the sides, then process again until smooth. Add the salt and several grinds of black pepper and pulse to combine. Add the Parmesan, if using, and pulse to combine. Pesto will keep in an airtight container in the fridge for about a week. To freeze, spread the pesto into an ice cube tray and cover with plastic wrap. Freeze until firm, then pop the cubes out into a resealable plastic bag where they will keep for a few months. Use two cubes for 8 ounces of pasta.

ABOUT BEANS

The convenience of canned beans can't be beat: pop the top, drain (or don't), and you're on your way. But if months of quarantine taught me anything, it was how to treat *dried* beans with the same time and respect I might offer a premium cut of meat.

Dried beans are an incredible value. Even a pound of the finest heirloom beans won't cost you more than $5.95. A pound of dried beans, cooked, equals four 15.5-ounce cans, meaning even the fanciest options won't cost you more than $1.50 per "can." Dried beans are also lighter weight. This may seem silly, but if you've ever tried a grocery run holding a baby on one hip and using a handheld basket, you know that even two cans of beans can be a real elbow breaker.

The following recipe is pretty stripped down: onion, garlic, olive oil, a few herbs if you have them. Play around with aromatics. Add a chili, whole or a pinch of flakes. Cook the beans in broth if you have it. Add other herbs (a few sprigs of fresh parsley, thyme, rosemary, cilantro, mint, or oregano all add wonderful flavor and aromas). Omit the garlic if you hate it; double if you love it. Same goes for the onion. Add a carrot or celery stalk to flavor the cooking liquid. Got leftover bacon fat from breakfast? Use that instead of the olive oil. Adapt your beans depending on what's available to you. Really, you could cook them in water alone, just don't skip the salt.

Depending on the freshness of your dried beans and the type of beans themselves, cooking times will vary. "Fresh" is defined by the bean experts at Rancho Gordo (a specialty producer and seller of heirloom beans based in Napa County,

California) as no more than two years old, but whatever you're starting with, soaking ahead will speed up cooking time.

When you start to check them for doneness, know that certain varieties (like pinto beans) will have a creamy interior, making them excellent for mashing onto tortillas or into dips, while others (like dried lima beans) will be slightly fluffier, almost mashed potato–like inside their skins. Chickpeas should *just* give like a nicely steamed carrot; that is, they should be tender but still hold their shape. Taste about five beans from different areas of the pot to make sure all are evenly cooked. If you're not sure, just keep simmering. Worst-case scenario: the beans will lose their shape, but they'll still be good to eat. Let the beans cool in their liquid before storing. I divide my beans into pint-size containers. That way I can use a pint wherever a 15.5-ounce can might be called for.

Use these beans in the Lentil Parmesan Soup (page 208) in place of the lentils or the Garlic and Oil Beans (page 203). Simmer them into a quick cassoulet (page 255) or add spices for a dish inspired by dal. Smash them onto tortillas or add them to salads. Or simply eat them as is, topped with pesto (page 100), Slow-Roasted Tomatoes (page 79), or a drizzle of oil and smattering of salt.

ADAPTABLE
BEANS

Active time: 10 minutes (plus soaking) | **Total time: 2 hours** | **Makes about 8 cups**

1 pound dried beans, rinsed and picked over for any pebbles or grit, soaked overnight

1 large onion (any color), unpeeled and quartered

1 head garlic, halved crosswise

¼ cup olive oil

Several sprigs fresh parsley, thyme, rosemary, cilantro, mint, and/or oregano

2 tablespoons kosher salt

Freshly ground black pepper

Place the beans and their soaking liquid in a large heavy-bottom pot. Add the onion, garlic, oil, herbs, salt, several grinds of black pepper, and enough cold water to cover the beans by an inch or two. Bring the beans to a simmer, reduce the heat to medium-low, and cook, stirring occasionally, until the beans are tender, 30 minutes (lentils, great northern beans) to 2 hours (gigante beans, dried limas) depending on the size and freshness of the beans, tasting several to check. Remove from the heat and let cool. Divide the beans among four pint-size containers and refrigerate for up to 5 days or freeze up to 3 months.

This recipe makes the equivalent of four 15.5-ounce cans.

DATE:
CONTENTS:

WHOLE WHEAT CUMIN
FLATBREADS

Active time: 45 minutes | Total Time: 45 minutes | Makes 8

Flatbreads exist the world over, from tortillas, pita and Ethiopian injera to Armenian lavash and Norwegian lefse. I am a lover of all and an expert in none. But I'm a committed student: I've made a lot of these breads over the years, and it's pretty cool to see how slight variations in flour-to-fat ratios or cooking technique can make the same ingredients taste totally unique. When I started writing this recipe, I intended to make a simple homemade flour tortilla—flour, fat, salt, water. But then I added whole wheat flour, traditional in Indian flatbreads like roti and chapatis. You can make these with a combo of all-purpose and whole wheat flours or with all of one or the other. I tried some with whole cumin seed, which I really like, but if you don't, it isn't necessary. Sometimes they puff while you cook them—very exciting! But they'll still be delicious if they don't. Eat them warm with a little butter, alongside stewed beans, soup, or salad. They're sturdy enough as a base for crispy lamb (page 248) but thin enough to use like tortillas for tacos or quesadillas.

I cup all-purpose flour

½ cup whole wheat flour or all-purpose flour

1½ teaspoons cumin seeds, optional

I teaspoon kosher salt

½ teaspoon baking powder

¼ cup olive oil or vegetable oil, or other fairly neutral flavored oils

½ cup warm water

Unsalted butter, melted, for brushing

Combine flours, cumin seeds, if using, salt, and baking powder in a medium bowl. Add oil and water to the flour mixture and stir until almost incorporated. Turn dough out onto the counter and knead until smooth and elastic, about I minute.

Using a knife, cut dough into eight pieces. Roll each piece between your hands into a ball, then let rest 5 minutes.

Using a rolling pin, roll each ball into about an 8-inch circle. Heat a large cast-iron skillet over medium-high heat. Working with one round at a time, add it to the skillet and cook undisturbed until bubbles start to form and the dough starts to look opaque around the edges, about I minute. Flip the dough, brush with butter, and cook I to 2 minutes more.

Transfer flatbread to a dish towel, cover, and keep warm while you make the rest.

Store cooled flatbreads in a resealable plastic bag at room temperature for a day, in the refrigerator for a week, or freeze for up to 3 months. Defrost at room temperature for about 15 minutes. Reheat in a hot skillet or over a low flame on a gas stovetop, flipping, until warm.

PIE DOUGH

For me, finding a disk of flaky pastry in the freezer is like holding a winning lotto ticket. Or so I imagine. The fantasies start flooding in—sweet or savory? Paris or Hawaii? Pie or cookie? Vintage Vette or brand-new Benz? It holds unlimited possibilities.

I've been making and using the exact same pie dough recipe forever. I learned it in culinary school, or maybe it was an old cookbook. I can't be sure. It's a classic ratio of flour, butter, salt, and cold water. I've tried dozens of other methods, but none are as reliable (or as easy to measure) as this simple formula.

All the recipes in this book that call for pie dough can be made with store-bought dough. But the homemade stuff is buttery and flaky and so far superior to the store-bought version that I encourage you to make it yourself. At least once.

I've taught a lot of people how to make pie dough, from novice home bakers to professional cooks, and the most common mistake people make is overworking the dough. Have a light touch. You're aiming for a shaggy mass of buttery, floury bits. Then, gently press these together until the pieces adhere to each other. Take it too far and your dough will feel like Play-Doh. I understand the impulse: Play-Doh is awesome! And easy to work with. But you're not supposed to eat it.

For the most tender results, I suggest you make pie dough by hand, using your fingers to work the butter into the flour rather than a machine. I don't always have the time and patience for this, but if today you do, proceed by hand. If not, use a food processor and don't worry about it. It'll be great.

Use the dough to make the Seeded Crackers (page 274), the Sparkly Jam and Nut Tart (page 307), or of course to bake your favorite pie. Here's a bonus: roll the dough to about ⅛-inch thickness, dust with cinnamon and sugar, and cut into strips. Bake at 350°F until golden and irresistible smelling. Savor them while you check the Powerball numbers.

GO-TO PIE DOUGH

Active time: 15 minutes | Total time: 15 minutes (plus chilling) | Makes 2 disks

2½ cups all-purpose flour

1 teaspoon kosher salt

2 sticks cold unsalted butter, cut into half-inch pieces

½ cup cold water

TO MAKE BY HAND

Combine the flour and salt in a large bowl. Add the butter and toss the pieces to coat in the flour. Using your fingers, work the butter into the flour by squeezing and rubbing it into the flour. Keep going until the mixture feels more like sand than flour and you have some pea-size bits of floured butter remaining.

Grab a fork. Gradually drizzle the water around the bowl, using the fork to stir it gently to incorporate. Squeeze a small handful of dough in your hand. If it sticks together easily, you're done. If not, add a little more water, mix with the fork, and check again.

TO MAKE IN A FOOD PROCESSOR

Combine the flour and salt in the bowl of a food processor and pulse to combine. Add the butter and pulse twenty times. The butter should be a little pebbly and sandy. Place the water in a liquid measuring cup (or some other container that it's easy to pour from). Gradually add the water, *pulsing* the machine as you go (this does not mean keep it running) until you see the dough just start to come together at the bottom of the processor bowl.

GO-TO
PIE DOUGH

TO FINISH

Dump the mixture onto the counter and using a knife or bench scraper divide the pile in half. Transfer each smaller pile to a large piece of plastic wrap. Using the plastic wrap and your hands, lift the wrap over the edges of the mixture and press the dough together. Continue to do this, rotating the plastic as you go, until the dough starts to hold shape (disk or rectangle totally OK). Wrap in another layer of plastic wrap, then refrigerate at least 2 hours and up to 4 days, or freeze up to 3 months. Defrost in the fridge overnight before using.

> Use the plastic wrap to gather the shaggy pieces together, using your knuckles to help press dough into a disk.

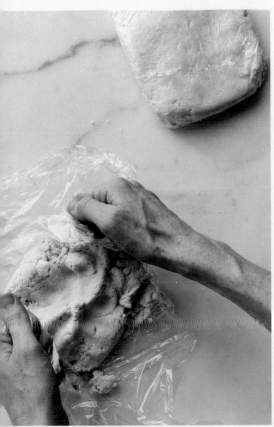

NUTS FOR NUTS

Adding toasted nuts to a recipe is one of those threefold additions we glorified home cooks love. By adding just one ingredient you can level up flavor, texture, and make something kinda pretty.

I like to buy my nuts whole and raw, but if you prefer pecan halves and pieces, say, or sliced almonds instead, that's cool, too. Either way, I prefer toasting them myself so I can really take them to a golden edge. It's also cheaper. Because they require an extra step in the preparation and packaging process, toasted nuts can be more expensive than raw ones.

Lots of recipes will suggest you toast nuts in a skillet on the stovetop. I've tried this a hundred times, and every time I end up mad. Cashews turn golden in spots and stay raw in the middle, pecans brown unevenly. The only surefire way to toast nuts thoroughly and evenly is in the oven, at 350°F. You want nuts to be golden all the way through—take a bite to check the inside to be sure.

Nuts are full of natural oils. That's one of the qualities that makes them so good for us. But oils go rancid under less than ideal conditions like fluctuations in temperature, moisture, etc. If you're unsure about your kitchen's climate, or you only use nuts on your Thanksgiving sweet potatoes, stick your nuts in the freezer. You can freeze them toasted or untoasted. Either way, they'll taste great through several holiday seasons.

As with so many pantry staples, once you get used to having toasted nuts around you'll think of endless ways to incorporate them. Chopped (or whole), they add crunch to salads, texture to simple tarts, and flavor and richness to regular cookie dough.

Here's one more hot tip I learned from a restaurant chef. While they're still warm, toss as many nuts as you need for a recipe in a little bit of olive oil and season with salt and pepper. Use this technique wherever nuts are added at the last minute, as a garnish or salad topper. They just taste better. Small thing, huge payoff. Just like toasted nuts themselves.

> If you get unpeeled hazelnuts, toast, then wrap in a clean dishtowel and set aside for a few minutes. Rub vigorously with the towel and the loose skins will come right off.

TOASTED NUTS

Active time: 2 minutes | Total time: 15 minutes | Makes however many you wish

Take them to the edge: deeply browned. Don't be scared.

Raw nuts such as almonds, pecans, walnuts, hazelnuts, or cashews

Preheat the oven to 350°F. Spread the nuts in a single layer on a rimmed baking sheet. Bake until fragrant and golden throughout (you may need to cut or bite into one to check), 12 to 15 minutes. Let cool, then transfer to a resealable plastic bag or other airtight container. Use within a couple of weeks or store in the freezer for a few months.

ALL-PURPOSE STREUSEL

Active time: 10 minutes | Total time: 10 minutes (plus chilling) | Makes about 1½ cups

I like to think I have medium to strong willpower. But when presented with crumb topping of any kind—a delicately sugared muffin, oat-studded fruit crumble, or the dense strata of a New York–style coffee cake—I cave right quick.

Before I started working on this book, streusel wasn't something I kept in the freezer all the time. I'd make the specified amount for a recipe, then stand over the finished product eating the biggest crumbs straight from the just-baked cake.

But while working on the Old-School Coffee Cake recipe (page 141), I did some lazy math and ended up with too much streusel, as if there could be such a thing. I stuck the leftovers in the freezer and promptly forgot about them. When I unearthed the frosty container weeks later, I thought Hmm, these bread crumbs look weird. I decided to taste them to find out what happened. What joy to discover these brown bits were not forgotten bread crumbs, but buttery brown sugar streusel.

Few items inspire the creative brainstorm that followed: I could crumble it over muffins, or pile it on halved peaches before baking. I could sprinkle it over banana bread batter (page 292) or maybe pumpkin pie. I could even spread it out on a sheet and bake it until firm, then crumble it over ice cream or pancakes, or layer it with whipped cream and fruit.

But if you want to use this streusel solely for the Old-School Coffee cake, that's as good a reason as any to have it at the ready.

1 cup all-purpose flour

1 cup light or dark brown sugar

1 teaspoon cinnamon

½ teaspoon kosher salt

1 stick (½ cup) unsalted butter, melted

Using a fork, mix the flour, brown sugar, cinnamon, and salt in a medium bowl. Add the melted butter and stir until evenly combined. Let cool, then transfer to an airtight container. Refrigerate up to a week or freeze up to 3 months.

PART 3

WHAT TO COOK

In this section, all your prep pays off. With a stocked and ready pantry and a handful (or more!) of your Pantry+ Ingredients, you'll be set up to make these fast, easy, delicious meals without a ton of stress. They're flexible, too, so if you have one ingredient instead of another, I've listed tons of variations where I've found it helpful. They might inspire you to dig into your own pantry and put your spin on things.

BREAKFAST

You're either a breakfast person or not. I must eat breakfast: left unfed I become truly awful company by 10 a.m. After two decades of casually surveying my adult peers, I find most breakfast people, myself included, eat one, maybe two things on rotation every workday: cereal, yogurt, oatmeal, toast. Me? Oatmeal, toast. What follows are around twenty ideas to diversify your regular [Insert preferred breakfast here] with ingredients you already have around.

When the weekend comes, breakfast (or second breakfast if you have little kids you already ate with upon waking) can and should get slower, later, and maybe a bit more decadent. But it shouldn't require a special grocery run or any advanced planning. Whatever you do have scheduled—soccer games, back-to-back birthday parties, or (re)watching every season of *Mad Men* from start to finish—there are savory pancakes, crepes, or coffee cakes to help you ease into it. You'll be able to whip them up while you're still in your PJs.

MAPLE COCONUT GRANOLA

Active time: 5 minutes | Total time: I hour | Makes about 8 cups

There's a problem with this granola: it's too good and smells like freshly griddled pancakes. It takes just five minutes, but I can't make it too often because I'll eat the entire batch warm off the baking sheet. I prefer maple syrup here, but you can use honey if you like. And while the addition of boxed cereal isn't necessary—a tip I learned from my friend and amazing cook, novelist Sanaë Lemoine—it adds an unexpected texture that makes this granola even more addictive. Proceed with caution.

3 cups rolled oats

1½ cups coconut chips

1½ cups pecans, walnuts, or almonds, roughly chopped

I cup Rice Krispies–type cereal or cornflakes, optional

¼ cup unsalted butter, olive oil, or vegetable oil

⅓ cup pure maple syrup

¼ cup light brown sugar

1½ teaspoons kosher salt

Preheat the oven to 300°F. Combine the oats, coconut, pecans, and cereal, if using, in a large bowl. Melt the butter in a small skillet or saucepan. Remove from the heat and whisk in the maple syrup, brown sugar, and salt. Pour over the oat mixture and stir until evenly coated. Transfer to a rimmed baking sheet and bake (no stirring!) until deeply browned, 45 to 50 minutes (it will likely look done after about 30 minutes, but keep going). Let cool completely. Then use a spatula (the pancake turner kind) to loosen the granola from the baking sheet in nice big clusters. Transfer to an airtight container. Granola will keep at room temperature up to 2 months.

BETTER OATMEAL

Active time: 5 minutes | Total time: 5 minutes | Serves 2 (but easily doubles or triples)

The secret to cooking oatmeal to tender perfection isn't actually a secret at all: it's on the back of the box. (The same is true for most grains. I often wonder why so many people are googling "how to cook rice," when presumably the directions are right in front of them. Maybe they bought it in bulk?) I encourage you to use the package directions and suggested ratios when they're offered. A whole team of food scientists and recipe developers likely tested under all sorts of varied conditions and altitudes and decided that ratio was ideal for this product.

However, there is a secret to this oatmeal. I make a slight adjustment to the back-of-the-oatmeal-box recipe. I use the suggested ratio of oats to liquid but, instead of combining them first, I bring the liquid to a boil alone, then add the oats. What results are chewy, well-defined grains you can eat right away or refrigerate for a couple of days. Reheat them with a splash of water, milk, or nondairy alternative on the stove or in the microwave.

1¾ cups water or milk

2 pinches kosher salt

1 cup old-fashioned rolled oats, not quick-cooking

Bring the water to a boil in a medium pot over high heat. Once boiling, add the salt and oats. Stir right away, then reduce the heat to low or medium-low so the oats are gently simmering. Simmer until tender but still chewy, 3 to 5 minutes. Drain any water if necessary. Top as you like. Here are some ideas:

BROWN BUTTER AND WALNUTS

Combine 2 tablespoons butter and ¼ cup roughly chopped walnuts in a small skillet over medium heat. Cook, stirring occasionally, until the butter is brown and nutty smelling and the walnuts are toasted, about 4 minutes. Sprinkle the hot oats with a little brown sugar (about 2 teaspoons per bowl) and pour the brown butter and nuts over top. Top with warm milk.

BANANA, HONEY, AND SESAME

Slice a banana and place in a bowl. Top with the hot oatmeal, a drizzle of honey, a teaspoon of toasted sesame seeds, and a sprinkle of cinnamon. Top with warm milk.

YOGURT AND JAM

Top the hot oatmeal with a couple of spoonfuls of plain yogurt and a spoonful of berry jam.

TAHINI, MAPLE, AND SALT

Top the hot oatmeal with a drizzle of tahini (or other nut butter thinned with a little water), a spoonful of maple syrup, and a pinch of flaky salt. Top with warm milk.

126

COCONUT-DATE

Top the hot oatmeal with 1 or 2 chopped pitted dates and a tablespoon each coconut flakes and chopped toasted nuts. Top with warm milk.

ALMOND BUTTER, HONEY, AND SALT

Swirl 2 tablespoons creamy almond butter (or whatever nut butter you like) into I cup plain yogurt. Drizzle with 2 teaspoons of honey and top with flaky salt.

CITRUS AND SEEDS

Top I cup plain yogurt with a few slices each of grapefruit, oranges, clementines, or tangerines and 2 teaspoons Mixed Seed Sprinkle (page 47).

YOGURT

What follows are a handful of easy-to-assemble, sweet and savory ideas that I hope will shake up your fruit-on-the-bottom yogurt routine. Many use the homemade pantry staples from Part 2 to add flavor and/or crunch. Play around with different combos and use whatever type of yogurt you prefer: Greek, Australian, Icelandic Skyr, or what have you.

SPICY CUCUMBER AND BLACK PEPPER

Top 1 cup plain yogurt with half a sliced Persian cucumber (about ½ cup). Drizzle with 2 teaspoons Quick Chili Oil (page 70); top with flaky salt and several grinds of black pepper.

OLIVE OIL AND ROASTED VEG

Top 1 cup plain yogurt with ½ cup leftover roasted vegetables. Drizzle with a tablespoon of olive oil and season with flaky salt and a few grinds of black pepper. Goes nicely with toast.

JAM AND CINNAMON

Top 1 cup plain yogurt with a heaping tablespoon Frozen Fruit Jam (page 86) or your favorite fruit preserves. Sprinkle with cinnamon and toasted coconut.

APPLES AND GRANOLA

Top 1 cup plain yogurt with half an apple, chopped, ¼ cup Maple Coconut Granola (page 125), and a drizzle of maple syrup.

SCALLION CORN CAKES

Active time: 30 minutes | Total time: 30 minutes | Makes 12 (serves 4)

I love the idea of those big diner breakfasts: eggs, bacon, and a pancake. Mostly because I really like bacon (or breakfast sausage) dragged through a pool of maple syrup. But I find most pancakes too soft and slightly too sweet to sit alongside an egg, no matter how it's cooked. Enter these hush-puppy-inspired corn cakes. Laced with scallions and cheddar cheese, they're savory enough to stand up against a runny yolk. And they're still good dipped in maple syrup. Omit the cheese and scallions for a more traditional johnnycake. Sweeter or more savory, they make a brilliant breakfast on their own or alongside bacon and eggs.

½ cup all-purpose flour

½ cup cornmeal

½ teaspoon baking powder

½ teaspoon baking soda

½ teaspoon kosher salt

Freshly ground black pepper

3 scallions, thinly sliced

½ cup sharp cheddar, shredded (about 2 ounces)

½ cup milk (any fat percentage will work)

1 large egg

2 tablespoons unsalted butter, melted, plus 2 tablespoons more for cooking

2 tablespoons vegetable oil

Maple syrup, for serving, optional

Whisk the flour, cornmeal, baking powder, baking soda, salt, and several grinds of black pepper in a large bowl. Add the scallions and cheddar and toss to combine. Make a well in the center of the dry ingredients and add the milk, egg, and 2 tablespoons melted butter; stir to combine.

Heat 1 tablespoon oil and 1 tablespoon butter in a large skillet over medium heat. Working in two batches, scoop 2 tablespoonfuls of batter onto the skillet. Cook, flipping once, until golden brown on both sides, about 3 minutes per side. Transfer to a wire rack. Repeat with remaining oil, butter, and batter. Serve with maple syrup for dipping or drizzling.

> If you really want to go for it, fry these cakes in rendered bacon drippings. Crisp the bacon in the skillet first, pour off all but a couple tablespoons of the fat, and proceed.

CINNAMON TOAST
CREPES

Active time: 40 minutes | Total time: 40 minutes | Makes 8

I once had the pleasure of hanging out/working with Ina Garten for a couple of weeks (long story, I'll tell you later). One night she told me that in her next life she'd open a crepe shop: "They're free!" she said, by which I think she meant crepes are mostly made of flour so the profit margins are very good. Which, of course, also makes them a perfect pantry recipe.

Crepe-making of any kind can be a little tricky at first. If your batter doesn't run easily around the pan, add a tablespoon of milk and whisk to combine. If you're still having trouble, continue adding milk a tablespoon at a time until the batter is thick but cooperative.

If this book thing doesn't work out, maybe I'll open a crepe shop, too. Ina, you in?

CINNAMON CREPES

I cup all-purpose flour

½ teaspoon kosher salt

½ teaspoon cinnamon

I¼ cups whole milk

2 large eggs

2 tablespoons melted butter, plus a little more for skillet

2 teaspoons pure vanilla extract

BROWN SUGAR BUTTER

6 tablespoons unsalted butter, at room temperature

6 tablespoons light or dark brown sugar

¾ teaspoon cinnamon

Pinch kosher salt

Whisk the flour, salt, and cinnamon in a large bowl. Make a well in the center of the dry ingredients and whisk in the milk, eggs, butter, and vanilla until super smooth. Let the batter rest while you make the Brown Sugar Butter.

Using a fork or the back of a spoon, smoosh together the butter, light brown sugar, cinnamon, and salt until smooth. Set aside.

Heat a medium nonstick skillet over medium heat. Brush with melted butter (a very little bit—*or* you can use a spent butter wrapper and just wipe that around the pan). Hold the skillet in one hand. Use your free hand to pour ¼ cup of the batter into the skillet. Immediately start tilting the skillet so the batter spreads and covers the entire bottom. Cook until the edges look dry and the bottom is golden brown in spots, about 2 minutes. Flip and continue to cook until dry on the other side, about I minute more. Transfer to a plate. Repeat with the remaining batter, stacking crepes as they are finished.

Spread the crepes with the sugar butter and roll or fold up. Serve warm or refrigerate, covered, up to a day. Pop them into the oven at 300°F to reheat.

DUTCH BABY WITH JAM

Active time: 10 minutes | Total Time: 30 minutes | Serves 2 to 4

When it comes to baking, many (this cook included) are guilty of skirting the preheat process and just throwing things into the oven at, like, 283°F or whatever. That's really only safe when reheating leftovers. This Dutch baby requires an oven at temperature and a hot skillet. Why? First, adding butter to an already hot pan creates a nonstick surface. Second, when the room temperature batter hits the hot buttered pan it creates steam (read: more lift), so the batter rises with impressive hills and the finished product slides out easily. Get your camera phones ready: this baby's a beauty.

⅔ cup milk (any fat percentage will work)

⅔ cup all-purpose flour

3 large eggs

1 tablespoon sugar

¼ teaspoon kosher salt

Zest of 1 lemon

5 tablespoons unsalted butter, divided

Frozen Fruit Jam (page 86) or Caramel Sauce (page 86), for serving

Preheat the oven to 425°F. Place a 10-inch cast-iron (or other oven-safe) skillet inside the oven to preheat, 10 full minutes. No cheating.

While the skillet gets hot, whisk together the milk, flour, eggs, sugar, salt, and lemon zest in a medium bowl. Whisk vigorously until no lumps remain (this could take about a minute—it should be really smooth).

Remove the skillet from the oven and add 4 tablespoons of butter, swirling until melted. Pour the batter into the skillet and quickly return it to the oven. Bake until golden and puffed up dramatically, 18 to 20 minutes.

Top with the remaining 1 tablespoon butter, tilting the skillet to help it melt all over and dollop with a few spoonfuls of jam.

GIANT FENNEL & RAISIN SCONE

Active time: 10 minutes | Total time: 1 hour | Serves 8

This recipe is inspired by Irish soda bread. More accurately, it is inspired by my desire to spread an inappropriate amount of butter on all breadlike things, especially Irish soda bread. You can eat it unadorned, preferably with a cup of Irish breakfast tea, but I highly recommend a healthy smear of slightly softened salted butter. I use fennel seed in the mixture to keep things from getting too sweet, but feel free to omit them if they aren't your thing. You can also substitute any dried fruit you like in place of the raisins. This is best eaten warm. Slice any leftovers and reheat in the toaster.

2½ cups all-purpose flour

½ cup whole wheat flour (or all-purpose flour)

½ cup sugar, plus 1 tablespoon for sprinkling

1 teaspoon baking soda

1 teaspoon baking powder

1 teaspoon kosher salt

1 cup raisins, dried apricots, or dried cherries, chopped raisin-size if necessary

1 tablespoon fennel seeds, caraway seeds, or rolled oats

1½ sticks (¾ cup) cold unsalted butter, cut into pieces, plus more for serving

1 cup whole milk

Preheat the oven to 350°F. Line a baking sheet with parchment paper. In a large bowl, whisk together the all-purpose flour, whole wheat flour, ½ cup sugar, baking soda, baking powder, and salt. Add the raisins and fennel seeds and whisk to combine. Add the butter and, using your fingers, work into the flour, pinching and squishing until the mixture is sandy.

Add the milk and use a fork to stir until evenly combined (the dough will be crumbly).

Dump the dough onto the prepared baking sheet into about an 8-inch circle, gently pressing and mounding the dough so it holds together. Sprinkle the top with the remaining 1 tablespoon sugar. Bake until golden and the scone sounds hollow when tapped with your finger, 45 to 50 minutes. Let cool slightly before cutting into slices or wedges. Serve warm with butter.

OLD-SCHOOL COFFEE CAKE

Active time: 20 minutes | Total time: I hour | Makes one 9-inch cake

This cake is some of my best work. But don't take my word for it. "All is Perfection. Quote me on that," said friend and fellow food editor Ananda Eidelstein after testing the recipe. "Best coffee cake I've ever had," said friend and neighbor Claire. She had a new baby at the time, though, and was probably delirious. (Delirious mom opinions count double.) As a lover of all things crumb topped, I think this coffee cake is the best. You can probably start it right this minute and be back from the corner store or closest supermarket (if necessary) by the time the butter is softened and the oven is preheated. Make it for yourself (it freezes well) or for a family or friendly gathering. I really believe in this cake! I hope you will, too.

FOR THE CRUMBS

I cup all-purpose flour

I cup light brown sugar

I teaspoon cinnamon

½ teaspoon kosher salt

I stick (½ cup) unsalted butter, melted and cooled, plus more for the cake pan

FOR THE CAKE

I stick (½ cup) unsalted butter, at room temperature

½ cup granulated sugar

2 large eggs

I cup all-purpose flour

½ teaspoon baking powder

½ teaspoon baking soda

½ teaspoon kosher salt

½ cup whole milk

Powdered sugar, optional, for serving

MAKE THE CRUMBS

Preheat the oven to 350°F. Brush a 9-inch-round cake pan with butter (or coat with nonstick spray). Using a fork, mix the flour, brown sugar, cinnamon, and salt in a medium bowl. Add the melted butter and stir until evenly combined. Place in the fridge while you make the cake.

MAKE THE CAKE

Using an electric mixer on medium-high, combine the butter and granulated sugar until light and fluffy, about 4 minutes. Add the eggs, one at a time, and beat to combine, scraping down the sides of the bowl as needed. Stir together the flour, baking powder, baking soda, and salt in a medium bowl. Add half the flour mixture to the butter mixture and beat to combine. Add the milk, beat to combine, then the remaining flour mixture. Beat until just incorporated.

Spread half the batter in the prepared pan and top with half the crumbs. Spread the remaining batter on top and scatter the remaining crumbs over the top. Bake until golden and risen and a toothpick inserted in the center of the cake comes out clean, 40 to 45 minutes. Let cool in the pan. Dust with powdered sugar, if using, and cut into wedges or squares.

OLIVE OIL MUFFINS

Active time: 10 minutes | Total time: 40 minutes | Makes 12

I love a freshly baked muffin, split and steaming like the ones in the old Country Crock commercials. (I encourage a rewatch. The talking hands, the innuendo, the enormous tubs of margarine: priceless!) But when a craving for a freshly baked muffin strikes, I don't like to wait very long. These adaptable one-bowl muffins come together in a snap. They call for olive oil, not butter (which means no waiting for butter to soften). I like the flavor olive oil imparts to the batter, but vegetable oil works just fine, too, if that's what you have. Both make for a tender, moist crumb. Make them as is and serve with butter, then try one of the variations on page 145.

1⅓ cups all-purpose flour

⅔ cup sugar

1 teaspoon baking powder

¼ teaspoon baking soda

½ teaspoon kosher salt

⅔ cup milk (preferably whole)

⅓ cup olive oil

1 large egg

Preheat the oven to 350°F. Line 12 standard muffin cups with paper liners. Whisk together the flour, sugar, baking powder, baking soda, and salt in a large bowl. Make a well in the center of the dry ingredients. Add the milk, oil, and egg and whisk to combine. Divide the batter among the muffin cups and bake until golden and springy when pressed, 25 to 30 minutes. Let cool slightly before serving.

VARIATIONS

CITRUS

Add I teaspoon lemon or orange zest and 2 tablespoons lemon or orange juice to the batter.

SPICED

Add I teaspoon cinnamon, ½ teaspoon ground ginger, and ½ teaspoon ground nutmeg to the dry ingredients.

BERRY

Fold I½ cups fresh or frozen berries into the batter and bake as directed (makes 15).

DOUGHNUT

Mix ½ cup granulated sugar with I teaspoon cinnamon in a shallow bowl. Brush the tops of warm muffins with melted butter and dip in the cinnamon sugar.

GLAZED

Whisk I cup powdered sugar with I to 2 tablespoons milk and a splash of pure vanilla extract until smooth. Dip tops of cooled muffins in the glaze, then invert onto a plate or cooling rack. Set aside until glaze sets.

EGG IN-A-HOLE

Active time: 5 minutes | Total time: 5 minutes | Serves I

You don't really need a recipe for this, but I wanted to remind you that an egg-in-a-hole (or egg-in-a-nest, egg-in-a-basket, or my favorite, a hole in one) is easy to make and eat. The first time I made one for my daughter, she looked at me and said, "You made this?" A win! They're fun just as they are, but take well to additions, like the Zing! Sauce (page 82), Quick Chili Oil (page 70), or Slow-Roasted Tomatoes (page 79).

I tablespoon unsalted butter

I large piece crusty bread, sliced about I inch thick (from the middle of the loaf is preferable)

I large egg

Flaky salt or one of the flavored salts on page 56

Freshly ground black pepper

Melt ½ tablespoon butter in a nonstick skillet over medium-high heat. While the butter is melting, cut a hole out of the center of the bread using a cookie cutter or a thin-rimmed glass.

Add the bread to the skillet. Crack an egg into the hole and cook, undisturbed, until the egg is set on the bottom and the underside of the bread is golden, about 2 minutes. Add the remaining ½ tablespoon butter to the skillet. When melted, flip the bread (a little egg might spill out, but that's OK). Continue to cook until the egg white is set, I to 2 minutes more. Season with a little salt and a few grinds of black pepper. To eat like a pro, dip the buttery toasted round in the egg to break the yolk.

HOW TO POACH
AN EGG

If you've got eggs, you've got a meal. The trick is to figure out how you like them and master that method.

No method is more intimidating to home cooks than poaching. But if you can boil (or simmer) water, you can poach an egg. One of the good things about eggs is that they're relatively inexpensive, so you can practice poaching without going broke. And you can still eat the mess-ups. Here's how to do it:

Bring a small pot of water to a simmer, *not* a boil. You should see bubbles rising from the bottom of the pot like bubbles in a glass of champagne. Line a plate with paper towels and set it next to the pot.

Crack a single egg into a cup. If you're cooking more than one egg, you need more than one cup. This might seem like an annoying extra step, but it ensures an easy dismount and small splash when it's time to slip your egg into the pot. And it gives you an opportunity to fish out any shell shrapnel. If tidy whites are a priority, crack your eggs into a fine mesh strainer first. Any thin whites will fall through the strainer, leaving the sturdier white and yolk behind. Once you've strained, transfer your eggs to the individual cups.

When you're ready to drop, give your simmering water a good stir. This will create a gentle whirlpool. Slip the egg from its cup into the water. You'll see it start to set and turn opaque almost immediately. Set a timer for 3 minutes.

When the timer goes off, the whites should be set and the yolk still runny. Use a slotted spoon to transfer the egg to the paper towel–lined plate to blot dry.

Pop a poached egg on top of a salad of sturdy greens (like the Roasted Potato Salad with Chorizo and Almonds page 252, float on top of Lentil Parmesan Soup (page 208), or slide on top of a bowl of spaghetti. Or, you know, buttered toast.

HOW TO
BOIL AN EGG

There are a lot of ways to boil an egg. One of the more common methods involves covering your eggs with cold water, bringing the water to a boil, then removing the pot from the heat, covering it, and setting it aside for however long you like your egg cooked. But no matter how many times I've tried—100? 120?—I have never been standing over a pot of water at the moment it came to a boil. If you're like me, try this instead:

Soft-boiled (for dipping toast soldiers): 4 minutes

Jammy yolk (for grain bowls or noodle soups): 6 to 7 minutes

Hard-boiled (for snacking, salads, or deviling): 10 minutes

Bring an appropriately sized pot of water to a boil. Then, carefully lower eggs in using a slotted spoon or small fine-mesh sieve. Set a timer accordingly (see left).

While the eggs are boiling, fill a bowl with ice and cold water. When the timer goes off, use the slotted spoon to lift the eggs out of the hot water and transfer them to the ice bath. Ignore them until they're cool to the touch. Hard-boiled eggs will keep in the fridge for a few days. The others I recommend eating the same day you cook them.

TOAST

If left unchecked, I would eat buttered toast every single morning. And afternoon and evening. It is my desert island food. In order to protect my arteries, I sneak some of the following non-butter options into the mix. I've included some suggestions for the types of bread to use, but generally they're all good on those rustic loaves that you slice yourself. If you don't have a favorite bread bakery nearby, look over by the deli section in your supermarket to see what they have to offer. Ideally, you'll find something sturdy with a crunchy, deeply browned crust. Slice the loaf about ¾-inch thick and toast until golden and sturdy. Then, try one of these:

BEANS ON TOAST

Top toasted sourdough with a generous scoop of warm Adaptable Beans (page 104) or Garlic & Oil Beans (page 203). Mash with a fork and season with flaky salt and freshly ground black pepper.

MUSTARD AND CHEESE

Spread a toasted baguette or other sturdy bread with a tablespoon or two of grainy mustard. Top with thinly sliced sharp white cheddar and freshly ground black pepper.

BUTTER AND SALT

Smear toast, any kind, with a generous slice of the best quality butter you can find. Season with flaky salt or one of the flavored salts on page 56.

TUNA AND RADISH

Spread about a tablespoon of mayonnaise on toasted crusty bread. Top with half a can of oil-packed tuna, breaking up into bite-size pieces. Top with a sliced radish, a squeeze of lemon, and a drizzle of olive oil. Season with flaky salt and freshly ground black pepper.

YOGURT AND SPICES

Slather a piece of toasted whole grain sandwich bread with a couple tablespoons of Greek yogurt. Top with ½ teaspoon Za'atar Blend (page 52) and season with flaky salt.

BACON SANDWICH

Cook the bacon: arrange in a single layer on a rimmed baking sheet. Bake at 400°F until crisp, 15 to 20 minutes. Drain on a paper towel–lined plate. Generously butter two pieces of toast, preferably cinnamon-raisin. Top one slice with a few pieces of crispy bacon, then top with the other slice.

FRICO-FRIED EGGS

Active time: 5 minutes | Total time: 5 minutes | Serves 1

I was thirty-eight years old before I had a Frico-fried egg. (Frico is the Italian name for crispy baked—or fried—Parmesan cheese.) I have no idea how I missed them. I always have eggs in the fridge, and Parmesan, too. I am not one to give life advice (except on cooking, obviously), but when it comes to these cheesy, lacy-edged eggs, I have two words: don't wait.

¼ cup grated Parmesan (packed if grated on a Microplane)

2 large eggs

Kosher salt and freshly ground black pepper

Heat a nonstick skillet over medium-low heat. Add the cheese and spread to about a 5-inch round. Cook until the cheese is melted, about 30 seconds. Crack the eggs on top of the cheese and season with salt and a few grinds of black pepper. Cook, undisturbed, until the whites are set and the yolks are still runny (feel free to flip if you want a firmer yolk), 3 to 4 minutes.

Try these crispy cheesy eggs over grits (page 199) with a side of Long-Cooked Greens (page 74).

FLUFFY OMELET

Active time: 5 minutes | Total time: 5 minutes | Serves 2 to 4

I lived without a microwave for a long time. It was not that big a deal—I know how to reheat rice in a pot (just add a splash of water), and I drink my coffee fast enough that it rarely needs reheating. But now that I have a microwave, I'm not sure how I ever lived without one, especially as a parent to young kids. You can reheat leftovers in like two minutes! And there's no need to wash another pot. Plus, you can make the fastest, fluffiest omelet without ever turning on the stove. It's a free-form, McMuffin-inspired situation, perfect for breakfast sandwiches, tacos, or emergency meals for kids or adults.

2 eggs

Pinch kosher salt

Freshly ground black pepper, optional

2 to 3 tablespoons (eyeball this) grated or crumbled cheese, optional

Place the eggs, salt, a few grinds of black pepper, and the cheese, if using, in a microwave-safe bowl and whisk with a fork to combine. Microwave on high until puffed and just cooked through, 1 to 2 minutes. Let cool slightly before serving.

A fluffy omelet right at home on a split Buttery Biscuit (page 194). Bacon and extra cheese optional.

BREAKFAST
QUESADILLAS

Active time: 10 minutes | Total time: 10 minutes | Serves 1 to 2

This decadent breakfast is best made to order. But if you're quesadilla-ing for a crowd, go ahead and double or triple the recipe. Then, to ensure things stay warm and melty for everyone, set the first few quesadillas, unadorned, on a rack set inside a rimmed baking sheet and place in a low oven (about 250°F) while you assemble and cook the rest. And please don't feel pressured to eat this in the morning. The only thing that makes it "breakfast" is the egg. It's awesome any time of day.

1 tablespoon vegetable oil

1 large egg

2 ounces shredded cheddar, Monterey Jack, pepper Jack, or other good melting cheese

2 flour or corn tortillas

Sliced avocado, Out-of-Season Salsa (page 82), Quickled onions or chilies (page 66), yogurt or sour cream, and/or lime wedges for serving

Heat the oil in a large nonstick skillet over medium-high heat. Once it's hot, fry the egg as you like, (sunny-side up or over-medium preferred). Transfer to a plate.

Scatter the cheese over the tortilla and top with the 1 remaining tortilla. Add to skillet and cook, flipping once, until golden brown on both sides, 1 to 2 minutes per side. Transfer to a plate and top with the egg, avocado, salsa, pickled onions, etc.

MATT'S SOFT SCRAMBLE

Active time: 5 minutes | Total time: 5 minutes | Serves 1 or more

I make scrambled eggs like the ones I grew up with: beaten with a handful of shredded yellow cheddar and several shakes of Worcestershire sauce, then generally overcooked using high heat, and distractions, until very dry.

My husband's eggs are the opposite. He starts with a knob of butter in a nonstick—preferably ceramic—skillet. He lets it melt slowly over moderate heat. He seasons the eggs lightly with salt and slowly pours them into the pan. With a sturdy heat-safe spatula, he patiently sweeps, nudges, and waits until the eggs are just set. They are far better than mine. Is it the extra butter? Maybe. The low, slow heat? For sure. Or is it simply the care and attention turned toward a simple task? Yes, that, too.

2 eggs per person

Kosher salt and freshly ground black pepper

2 tablespoons unsalted butter

Beat the eggs in a medium bowl until well blended and season with salt and a few grinds of black pepper.

Melt the butter in a large nonstick skillet over medium heat. Add the eggs and, using a heat-safe spatula, gently push the eggs away from you toward the far side of the skillet in about three moves. Sweep the spatula around the edge of the skillet to gather any setting egg toward the center. Repeat these moves as many times as it takes until the eggs are just set (they'll continue to cook as they rest), usually about 2 minutes. Season with a little more salt and pepper if you like.

GREENS
GRITS & EGGS

Active time: 10 minutes | Total time: 10 minutes | Serves 2

I prefer a sweet breakfast. For a professional cook, this is terribly uncool—my peers are always talking about starting the day with brothy fish soups or spicy sautéed lentils. What can I say? I like muffins. But I know the savory breakfast contingent is strong and opinionated. For you I offer this little combo platter built with things you've already learned (or will soon learn) how to make. A scoop of creamy grits topped with garlicky long-cooked greens and a crispy frico-fried egg (or whatever style egg you prefer). It's a satisfying breakfast, especially on cold winter days, even for me.

1½ cups Sweet Potato Grits (page 199), warmed

1 cup Long-Cooked Greens (page 74), warm or room temperature

2 Frico-Fried Eggs (page 152)

Lemon-Sesame Salt (page 56), optional

Top the warm grits with the greens, eggs, and a sprinkle of Lemon-Sesame Salt, if using.

SALAD & VEGGIES

In an ideal world, we'd eat vegetables every night. But the washing and the chopping can sometimes be too much to bear (I've been there). The salads and vegetable sides in this chapter keep ingredients and prep time to a minimum—there is very little chopping required. They're fast and easy enough to throw together alongside one of the mains that follow. Or, to make one of these a meal in and of itself, put an egg on it and serve with toast.

HOW TO MAKE A SALAD

These days salads can be made of just about anything—grains, fruits, eggs, Jell-O. What a time to be alive! For the sake of this page, the salad in question is a green one. Keep these elements in the pantry and top of mind, to throw together a more satisfying salad.

CRUNCH

For me, some crunch is always desirable in a salad. That can come from the lettuce itself or other raw vegetables. Chopped celery, sliced radishes or beets, shaved fennel or carrot ribbons are all good choices. They're also lovely to look at. Thinly sliced apple or a firm pear add sweetness, while chopped toasted nuts, croutons, or crispy fried shallots are salad-friendly Pantry+ ingredients worth playing around with.

DRESSING

Keep the flavor and texture of your base in mind when deciding on a dressing. Tender mild leaves? Use a lightweight tangy dressing like the Garlicky Lemon Dressing (page 60) or Sesame-Ginger Dressing (page 61). Sturdier crunchy leaves and vegetables can handle creamier options.

CONTRAST

A little something extra adds contrast, whether that's for texture, color, or flavor. When a base is crispy or crunchy, add something rich and creamy like avocado, feta, or beans. Softer bases need crunch. Chopped Quickles (page 66), Cheese Crispies or the Mixed Seed Sprinkle (page 47) perk things up in all three categories in one go.

BASE

Focus on leaves with great texture and/or big flavor. Romaine, torn kale, and iceberg, for example, offer superior crunch. Bitter greens like endive, escarole, or radicchio add interesting flavors. Unexpected options like rainbow chard and mustard or collard greens can be eaten chopped or thinly sliced into ribbons, too. And don't forget about cabbage! It's not just for slaw. If you have the time, wash and dry your lettuce as soon as you get home from the store so they're ready to go when you're ready to eat. Though the cabbage can wait (and wait).

LITTLE GEMS W/ RANCH & SEEDS

Active time: 5 minutes | Total time: 5 minutes | Serves 4

Let's be honest: this salad is a showcase for the dressing. Let it shine! When the dressing is the star, I like to build a salad like nachos, in layers, so every leaf gets some attention. There's nothing sadder than pulling a naked nacho from the pile. Same goes for a plain piece of lettuce. I like Little Gem lettuces for this one. Once separated, their tightly bundled leaves are extra crunchy and petite so you can eat them like chips.

2 little gems or I romaine heart, leaves separated

4 celery stalks, thinly sliced

¼ cup Creamy Ranch, or other Creamy Dressings (page 62)

I tablespoon Mixed Seed Sprinkle (page 47) or chopped Toasted Nuts (page II6)

Flaky salt or flavored salt (page 56)

Freshly ground black pepper

Arrange half the lettuce leaves in a single layer on a large plate or platter. Sprinkle half the sliced celery on top. Spoon half the dressing over the leaves and celery and sprinkle with half the seeds. Season with salt and a few grinds of freshly ground black pepper. Repeat with the remaining leaves, celery, seeds, and dressing.

BITTER GREENS
W/ ORANGES & HAZELNUTS

Active time: 10 minutes | Total time: 10 minutes | Serves 4

A lot of people can be put off by bitter greens because they're so, well, bitter. Bite into a piece of especially spicy arugula or watercress all by itself and it might knock your socks off. But pair these bitter greens (or purples, as the case may be) with citrus and toasted nuts, and you've got a salad that will cleanse your palate, perfect for serving with anything on the heavier side: braised meats, spaghetti Bolognese, even a grilled cheese sandwich.

8 ounces bitter greens, such as radicchio, endive, arugula, or watercress, leaves separated

2 oranges, peeled and sliced crosswise, rounds pulled into bite-size pieces

½ cup toasted hazelnuts, almonds, or walnuts, chopped

2 teaspoons olive oil

Kosher salt and freshly ground black pepper

¼ cup Dijon Vinaigrette or Garlicky Lemon Dressing (page 60)

Toss the greens and oranges together in a large bowl. In a separate small bowl, toss the hazelnuts with the oil and season with salt and a few grinds of black pepper. Add the nuts and vinaigrette to the greens and toss to combine.

LEMON-LIME CABBAGE

Active time: 5 minutes | **Total time: 5 minutes** | **Serves 4**

I don't know how cabbage does it. On dozens of occasions I have found a half head in the back of the crisper that I was sure I used up a month ago. But there it is, crunchy and as good as new. If only I could be ignored for that long and still be so agreeable. This simple slaw is one of my favorite ways to eat cabbage, whether fresh from the market or discovered behind the carrots and kale. Eat it right away or wait a day or two for it to wilt a bit. It's delicious either way.

½ head red or green cabbage, cored and thinly sliced

3 tablespoons lemon or lime juice

2 tablespoons olive oil

½ teaspoon kosher salt

Freshly ground black pepper

Pinch sugar

Pinch crushed red pepper flakes, optional

In a large bowl, toss the cabbage with the lemon juice, oil, salt, several grinds of black pepper, and a pinch each of sugar and crushed red pepper flakes, if using. Eat right away or refrigerate for up to 2 days.

Want to change it up? Add some pickled raisins (page 62) and a handful of chopped toasted pecans.

SALT & VINEGAR CUCUMBERS

Active time: 5 minutes | **Total time: 5 minutes** | **Serves 4**

I ate some version of these simple crunchy cucumbers every other night from 1986 to 1997. I wasn't the pickiest eater on the planet, but my vegetable vocabulary took some time to expand. My mom usually used cider vinegar to dress the cukes, which can be pretty assertive. These days I prefer to use rice vinegar or white wine vinegar, or white balsamic if I have it, which are all pretty mild (but if cider vinegar is in your cupboard, proceed!). The superior crunch of English or Persian cucumbers is great here, but use whatever you have.

1 pound cucumbers, thinly sliced

1 shallot, thinly sliced

¼ cup rice vinegar or other mild vinegar

1 teaspoon kosher salt

Torn fresh dill, basil, parsley, or cilantro, optional

Combine the cucumber, shallot, vinegar, salt, and herbs, if using, in a medium bowl. Eat right away or set aside for up to a day.

> Try it topped with a handful of Garlic-Shallot Crunch (page 48).

CELERY SALAD WITH CHEESE, FRUIT & NUTS

Active time: 10 minutes | Total time: 10 minutes | Serves 4

Poor celery: relegated to stocks and soup bases, it never gets to take center stage. Not that there's anything wrong with supporting roles, but celery can do far more than serve as a landing pad for bugs on a log. This adaptable salad gives celery its star turn, but its real talent is its flexibility. Use any salty, assertive cheese you have on hand, whichever toasted nuts you prefer, and play around with sweet-tart fruits to see what you like best. Toss with one of the tangy dressings in part 2 (page 60) and serve alongside (or on top) of the Crispy Fried Chicken Cutlets on page 224.

8 celery stalks, chopped, plus some leaves

I sweet-tart apple or pear, cored and thinly sliced, or I cup grapes, halved, or ½ cup raisins (pickled or regular)

½ cup shaved Parmesan, pecorino, or sharp cheddar cheese

⅓ cup chopped toasted hazelnuts, almonds, or walnuts

¼ cup Dijon Vinaigrette, Garlicky Lemon Dressing, or Sesame-Ginger Dressing (page 61)

Flaky salt and freshly ground black pepper

In a large bowl, combine the celery, apple, Parmesan, hazelnuts, and vinaigrette. Taste and season with flaky salt and a few grinds of black pepper.

For a different take, skip the cutlets (shown on following page) and add some cooked drained beans or tuna to the salad.

TWO CITRUS SALADS

Active time: 15 minutes | Total time: 15 minutes | Serves 4

Whenever I'm invited to someone's place between January and March (when citrus fruit is at its best), I bring some variation of this salad. Depending on whether I'm asked to bring a "salad" or a "fruit," I'll make it more savory or keep it sweet. If you already have pickled onions (page 66) in your fridge, you can use those in place of the shallots.

BASE
1 grapefruit, peeled and sliced crosswise

1 navel orange, or 2 clementines or tangerines peeled and sliced crosswise

CITRUS W/ OLIVES & ONION
1 shallot, thinly sliced

½ teaspoon kosher salt

Freshly ground black pepper

2 tablespoons red wine vinegar

½ cup Castelvetrano olives, pitted and torn

2 tablespoons olive oil

Flaky salt or Chile-Lime-Cumin Salt (page 56), optional

CITRUS W/ NUTS & COCONUT
1/4 cup toasted nuts

2 tablespoons of toasted coconut flakes or Coconut Crunch (page 47)

2 tablespoons olive oil

Flaky salt

FOR CITRUS WITH OLIVES AND ONION (SAVORY)
Place the shallot in a small bowl, season with salt and several grinds of black pepper. Cover with the vinegar and set aside while you prep the citrus and olives.

Arrange the grapefruit and orange on a platter. Scatter the olives and shallots over the top, drizzling with a little of the shallot vinegar and oil. Top with flaky salt.

FOR CITRUS WITH NUTS AND COCONUT (SWEET)
Arrange the citrus on a platter. Top with nuts and toasted coconut flakes, drizzle with the oil, and top with flaky salt.

PITA CHIPS WITH TOMATOES & CUCUMBERS

Active time: 15 minutes | Total time: 15 minutes | Serves 4 to 6

There was a time when I was so obsessed with Stacy's pita chips that my coworkers joked I was getting paid to snack on them around the office. I'm still a fan, but I've diversified my snack profile since then. I will, however, find excuses to use them whenever possible, whether crushed in place of bread crumbs in meatballs or to coat a chicken cutlet. With a nod to fattoush—a zesty Lebanese salad of crunchy chopped vegetables and toasted pita—-this salad is one of my favorite ways to use them and one of the easiest. The chips will soften ever so slightly when doused in the dressing and then slowly succumb over the next day or two, at which point they are chewy and interesting. Any longer than that and they get kind of soggy, so eat up.

1 English or 2 Persian cucumbers, sliced

1 pint cherry or grape tomatoes, halved or 1 beefsteak, cut into wedges

1 teaspoon kosher salt

Freshly ground black pepper

1 tablespoon red wine vinegar

1 garlic clove, grated

1 tablespoon Za'atar Blend (page 52) or store-bought za'atar

2 tablespoons olive oil, plus more for drizzling

1 cup lightly crushed pita chips

1 cup fresh parsley and/or mint leaves (or cilantro or basil)

In a medium bowl, toss together the cucumber and tomatoes with the salt and a few grinds of black pepper; set aside until the tomatoes start to give up some of their juices, about 5 minutes or so. Add the vinegar, garlic, Za'atar, oil, pita chips, and herbs and toss to combine.

> You can make this with all tomatoes or all cucumbers, or add some sliced feta or chickpeas to make it a meal. Just don't skip the chips.

PEAS W/ FRIED ONIONS & LEMON

Active time: 20 minutes | Total time: 20 minutes | Serves 4

I will often run frozen peas under hot water, toss them with a little salt, and slide them on to my son's high chair tray. He likes 'em! But most nights, that's not quite enough for me. Even at their best, I find plain peas to be kind of starchy. Dousing them in melted butter or olive oil helps, but fried onions and chopped lemon really make them sing. Don't be intimidated by the whole lemon in the mix here. The bitter tang of the peel and all cuts through the sweet richness of the sizzled onions and potential starchiness of the peas. This recipe works with anything frozen and niblet-size. I prefer peas, but shelled edamame and corn are great options, too.

¼ cup olive oil

1 yellow onion, thinly sliced

10 ounces frozen peas, rinsed to thaw

½ lemon, seeded and finely chopped (peel and all)

1 teaspoon kosher salt

Freshly ground black pepper

Heat the oil in a medium skillet over medium-high heat. Add the onion and cook, stirring occasionally, until dark brown (really dark brown in some spots), 6 to 8 minutes. Stir in the peas and cook until heated through, about 1 minute. Remove from the heat, stir in the lemon, and season with the salt and a few grinds of black pepper.

ANY VEGETABLE
FRITTERS

Active time: 30 minutes | Total time: 30 minutes | Serves 4 (makes 18)

I originally made these latke-like fritters, a pancake of mixed sturdy vegetable odds and ends, in the hopes that my daughter would eat other vegetables besides nearly burned broccoli and raw carrot sticks. Depending on the day, she'll try them. Either way, they're a great way to use up random veggie bits and pieces, like abandoned onion halves, or use the less loved, like broccoli stems. You can use traditional russet potatoes in the mix, but they are so like french fries it's sort of missing the point here, which is fewer french fries, more other vegetables. I like them topped with or dipped in a little yogurt, but any of the Creamy Dressings (page 62) would be delicious accompaniments. If you have a food processor with a grating disk, this is a great time to use it.

2½ cups coarsely grated vegetables, such as carrots, zucchini, sweet potatoes, butternut squash, beets, broccoli stems, or parsnips

I small (or half a large) yellow or red onion, coarsely grated

¼ cup all-purpose flour

¾ teaspoon kosher salt

½ teaspoon ground coriander

Freshly ground black pepper

I large egg

¼ cup vegetable oil, plus more as needed

Yogurt and chopped fresh herbs, such as parsley, cilantro, mint or chives, for serving

In a medium bowl, toss the shredded vegetables and onion with the flour, salt, coriander, and several grinds of black pepper. Crack the egg into the bowl and mix until evenly combined.

Heat the oil in a large skillet over medium-high heat. Working in batches so you don't overcrowd the skillet, drop rounded tablespoonfuls of the vegetable mixture into the hot oil and cook, flipping halfway through, until golden brown on both sides, 5 to 6 minutes per batch. Transfer to a wire rack lined with a paper towel. Repeat with the remaining vegetable mixture, adding another tablespoon or two of oil to the skillet if it looks dry. Serve topped with yogurt and chopped herbs.

Any untopped, cooled fritters can be stored in the refrigerator for up to 3 days or frozen for up to a month. Reheat in the oven at 400°F until warmed through, about 10 minutes.

SPICY SWEET
BRUSSELS SPROUTS

Active time: 10 minutes | Total time: 30 minutes | Serves 4

My mom often recounts horror stories of being served boiled Brussels sprouts as a kid. Pale and squidgy (and not great smelling, either), they were a challenge to enjoy. It turned her off Brussels sprouts for decades. But roasted and sauced in a salty-sweet mixture of soy and honey, these Brussels sprouts convert even lifelong haters. By some combination of magic and science, this exact same preparation works with green beans. You could even use half Brussels sprouts and half beans. In both scenarios, the vegetables get very tender and very brown. And in any case the sauce is easy and delicious and could be spooned over lots of different cooked vegetables, drizzled over rice, or tossed with boiled noodles.

I pound Brussels sprouts or green beans, trimmed (Brussels sprouts halved if huge)

2 tablespoons vegetable oil

3 tablespoons soy sauce or tamari

3 tablespoons honey or maple syrup

I tablespoon cider vinegar

I teaspoon sambal or Sriracha or ½ teaspoon crushed red pepper flakes, plus more to taste

Chopped toasted nuts, sesame seeds or Coconut Crunch (page 47), or Garlic-Shallot Crunch (page 48), optional

Preheat the oven to 425°F. Toss the sprouts with the oil on a rimmed baking sheet. Roast, shaking the sheet halfway through, until deeply browned and tender, 20 to 25 minutes.

Meanwhile, combine the soy sauce, honey, vinegar, and sambal in a medium skillet. Bring to a simmer over medium-high heat, stirring occasionally, until slightly reduced and syrupy, 2 to 3 minutes. Remove from the heat.

Reheat the sauce, if necessary, add the vegetables, and toss to coat. Taste and add more sambal for more heat. Top with nuts, seeds, or crunch, if using.

Great with grilled or sautéed shrimp. Serve over rice.

183

STARCHY SIDES

A smart friend once told me that whenever she orders a take-out salad she always gets a side of mashed potatoes. That's because a salad all by itself rarely fills you up or feels like a meal. Enter carbs. Starchy sides like steamed rice, roasted potatoes, or a simple piece of toast can round out a meal easily and inexpensively. Plus these ingredients last almost forever in your pantry. Eaten in moderation, and if they agree with you, obviously, they help you feel satisfied and generally make my family less annoying dining companions. The following recipes are a great reminder of what all these ingredients can do for you.

DINNER TOAST

Active time: 5 minutes | Total Time: 5 minutes | Serves 4

Good bread—crusty on the outside, tender and chewy on the inside—is a truly wonderful way to round out a meal. Whether your sauce or soup needs sopping up, good bread is the perfect partner. But good bread is only really good as is for about twenty-four hours. After that it benefits from toasting and some pantry love. These three special toasts use ingredients you probably have around—like garlic, tomato paste, and Parmesan—to drastically upgrade a day-old loaf.

4 thick slices crusty bread

Olive oil (you really don't have to measure)

Kosher salt

Freshly ground black pepper

In an effort to make a pizza-like sauce without cracking a jar, my friend Jennifer came up with this savory combination. The olive oil mixture also makes a delicious dip for focaccia or other fresh loaves.

Arrange the bread on a rimmed baking sheet. Drizzle with the oil and season with a little salt and a few grinds of black pepper.

GARLIC TOAST
Broil the bread until golden, flipping halfway through, 1 to 2 minutes per side. Rub a peeled garlic clove all over each slice. Drizzle with a little more oil and add more salt if you like.

CHEESY TOAST
Broil the bread until golden on one side, about a minute. Flip and top each slice with 2 tablespoons finely shredded cheese (any kind, any combo). Broil until melted and bubbly, 1 to 2 minutes.

TOMATO TOAST
In a small bowl, mix together 1 tablespoon each tomato paste, balsamic vinegar, and olive oil. Broil the bread until golden on one side, about 1 minute. Flip and brush the untoasted side with the tomato mixture and broil until slightly darker and toasted around the edges, 1 to 2 minutes. Top with flaky salt or one of the flavored salts on page 56.

RICE TO THE RESCUE WITH NUTS & HERBS

Active time: 5 minutes | Total time: 5 minutes | Serves 4

For several summers I worked as a private chef for a family in the Hamptons, an enclave of ritzy beach communities on the east end of Long Island in New York. Most of the time I cooked for a lovely older couple, their children and grandchildren. But friends and acquaintances rolled through the house in sets like waves. You'll stay for lunch! *visitors were told.* Come for dinner! *they insisted. Ex-presidents, vegetarian children, kosher sons-in-law, exhausted candidates, campaign chairs observing halal—all were welcome. Which meant some fancy footwork on my part. This grain salad was a life raft for me whenever surprise guests joined the party. You can make it with whatever rice, grains, or nuts that you have around. And each time you change it up, it feels new. Make it as is and it's vegan (and pareve!). Add shaved Parmesan or sliced chicken to make it a meal.*

3 cups cooked rice or grains, such as brown rice, barley, farro, quinoa, or a mix (from I cup dry)

3 scallions, thinly sliced, or I shallot, finely chopped

3 tablespoons olive oil

Zest and juice of I lemon or 1½ tablespoons red or white wine vinegar

½ cup chopped toasted hazelnuts, almonds, pecans, and/or walnuts

½ cup chopped fresh parsley, basil, dill, and/or mint

½ cup golden raisins, dried cherries, or cranberries

½ teaspoon kosher salt

Freshly ground black pepper

Combine the rice, scallions, oil, lemon zest and juice, nuts, herbs, raisins, salt, and several grinds of black pepper in a large bowl and toss to combine. The salad can be made up to 2 days ahead (after that it is no less edible, but loses some of its brightness).

A FEW WAYS WITH
BOILED POTATOES

Having boiled potatoes ready to go can set you up for dozens of tasty sides.
Tossed in melted butter and Old Bay or smashed with a glug of olive oil and
chopped chives, they're a perfect side for grilled chicken, seared fish, or the
braised beef on page 247. These shortcut recipes round out dinner in a snap.

OVEN-CRUNCH POTATOES

Active time: 10 minutes | Total time: 40 minutes | Serves 4

¼ cup olive oil

Boiled potatoes (any kind, about 1½ pounds), cooled

½ teaspoon salt

Instant Aioli (page 83), for serving

2 scallions, thinly sliced

Flaky salt or one of the flavored salts on page 56, for serving

Turn the oven on to 425°F. Place the oil in an oven-safe skillet and stick it in the oven while it preheats, about 10 minutes. Using your hands, gently break the potatoes apart into bite-size pieces. Once the oil is hot, remove the dish from the oven and place on the stovetop. Carefully add the boiled potatoes and season with the salt, turning to coat in the hot oil. Return to the oven and roast, turning every 10 minutes, until golden, 30 to 35 minutes total. Spread the aioli on a platter and top with the potatoes, scallions, and more salt.

CRISPY SMASHED POTATOES

Active time: 15 minutes | Total time: 15 minutes | Serves 4

Boiled potatoes (small and waxy, 1½ pounds), cooled

3 tablespoons olive oil

3 tablespoon unsalted butter

Kosher salt

Small handful fresh sage leaves or oregano leaves, or 3 sprigs fresh thyme or rosemary

Freshly ground black pepper

Flaky salt or one of the flavored salts on page 56, optional

Gently flatten each potato by pressing it with the palm of your hand until it gives way but doesn't fall apart.

Heat 1 tablespoon oil and 1 tablespoon butter in a medium skillet over medium-high heat until the butter melts. Add the flattened potatoes, season with salt, and cook, flipping once, until golden and crispy on both sides, about 2 minutes per side. Transfer to a plate and repeat with 1 tablespoon each oil, butter, and the remaining potatoes.

Add the last 1 tablespoon oil and butter to the skillet and swirl to heat it up. Add the sage leaves and cook, swirling the skillet a little, until the leaves start to curl at the edges and become brittle, 30 seconds to 1 minute. Pour over the potatoes and season with several grinds of black pepper and flaky (or more kosher) salt.

COLD POTATOES
WITH MUSTARD & ONIONS

Active time: 10 minutes | Total time: 10 minutes | Serves 4 (but easily doubles)

Boiled potatoes (any kind, 1½ pounds), cooled

¼ cup olive oil

1 red or yellow onion, halved and thinly sliced

1 teaspoon kosher salt, divided

Freshly ground black pepper

3 tablespoons coarsely chopped parsley or chives

2 tablespoons red wine vinegar

2 tablespoons whole grain or Dijon mustard

Lightly crush the potatoes with your hands so the insides are exposed. Place in a large bowl.

Heat the oil in a medium pot or skillet over medium-high heat until shimmering. Add the onion and season with ½ teaspoon salt and several grinds of black pepper. Cook, stirring occasionally, until the onion is tender and dark brown in spots, 5 to 7 minutes. Remove from the heat.

Add onion and oil to the potatoes along with the parsley, vinegar, mustard, remaining ½ teaspoon salt, and more black pepper; toss to coat (it's OK if the potatoes break down a little more). This can be made up to 2 days ahead. Store in the fridge in an airtight container.

BUTTERY BISCUITS

Active time: 10 minutes | Total time: 40 minutes | Makes 8

Biscuits were one of the inspirations for this book. I always have the ingredients around, and every time I make them I can't believe something so delicious and crowd pleasing came from my pantry. Biscuits are a lesson in richness: of the buttery variety but also of possibility. Never has anything so special—warm and golden, split and saturated with salted butter—come from such humble beginnings.

2½ cups all-purpose flour

I tablespoon sugar

I tablespoon baking powder

I teaspoon kosher salt

½ teaspoon baking soda

I stick cold unsalted butter plus 2 tablespoons, melted, for brushing

I cup whole milk, buttermilk, or ¾ cup plain yogurt whisked with ¼ cup milk

Preheat the oven to 400°F with a rack in the upper third. Whisk together the flour, sugar, baking powder, salt, and baking soda in a large bowl. Using the large holes of a box grater, grate the butter directly over the flour mixture, stopping a couple of times to toss the butter into the dry ingredients to coat. Add the milk and use a fork to stir until shaggy.

Dump the dough onto the counter and press into a I-inch-thick rectangle. Fold the dough on top of itself a couple of times until all of the bits and pieces of flour are almost incorporated (a few stragglers are OK). Pat the dough to a I-inch thickness and cut into eight squares. Transfer to a parchment-lined baking sheet and brush with the 2 tablespoons butter.

Bake until golden and risen, 25 to 30 minutes.

VARIATIONS

HERB

Add ¼ cup finely chopped tender herbs such as parsley, basil, chives, or cilantro to the flour mixture before adding the milk. Bake as directed.

CHEESY

Add 1 cup shredded or crumbled cheese to the flour mixture before adding the milk. Bake as directed.

OLD BAY

While the biscuits are baking, mix 2 teaspoons Old Bay Seasoning with 2 tablespoons melted butter. Brush the warm biscuits all over with the Old Bay butter.

SHORTCAKE

Increase the sugar to ¼ cup. Bake the biscuits as directed. Let cool then split. Serve the shortcakes topped with whipped cream and/or ice cream and fresh berries.

SWEET POTATO GRITS

Active time: 15 minutes | Total time: 45 minutes | Serves 6

Grits are unsung pantry heroes if you ask me. They can go sweet, they can go savory; they can be a side or a breakfast; they're great à la minute, but make pretty awesome leftovers. This comforting side is the perfect excuse to use up random roasted vegetables that might be lurking in the back corner of the fridge, too. Baked sweet potatoes, roasted fall squash, even Long-Cooked Greens (page 74) turn a pot of buttery decadent grits into a slightly more sophisticated version of buttery decadent grits (if it ain't broke). Spread any leftovers in a cake pan and refrigerate overnight. When firm, cut into shapes (let kids punch out using cookie cutters) and panfry.

2 teaspoons kosher salt

1 cup grits (preferably not quick-cooking) or coarse-grind cornmeal or polenta

1 roasted sweet potato, mashed (about 1 cup), or 1 cup other leftover cooked vegetables

4 tablespoons unsalted butter

Freshly ground black pepper

Bring 5 cups of water to a boil in a medium pot over high heat. Add the salt and gradually whisk in the grits. Reduce the heat to low, cover, and cook, uncovering to whisk whenever you walk by or remember (a few times should do it) until the grits are very tender, 30 to 35 minutes.

Stir in the sweet potato, butter, and as much pepper as you like, until the butter melts and the grits are smooth and luxurious.

> A couple other ideas: Stir in two cubes of frozen Flexo-Pesto (page 100) or top with Slow-Roasted Tomatoes (page 79) and grated Parm.

TENDER SKILLET CORN BREAD

Active time: 10 minutes | Total time: 40 minutes | Serves 8

Boy, do y'all have opinions about corn bread. When I asked my Instagram friends if they wanted a Jiffy-style corn bread (to me that means golden, crumbly, in need of butter) or a cakelike version, the comment floodgates opened. This version is right in between. It has a little bit of sugar, which helps to tenderize the corn bread without making it too sweet. This is best eaten the day it's made, but leftovers are excellent split, toasted under the broiler or in the toaster oven, and topped with butter, butter and jam, butter and honey, or butter and butter.

1 cup milk (preferably whole)

1 tablespoon lemon juice

1½ sticks unsalted butter

1 cup all-purpose flour

1 cup stone-ground cornmeal

¼ cup sugar

1 tablespoon baking powder

1 teaspoon kosher salt

½ teaspoon baking soda

2 large eggs

Preheat the oven to 400°F. Combine the milk and lemon juice in a bowl or liquid measuring cup and set aside for 5 minutes. Ideally the milk will curdle a bit here; sometimes it's obvious and sometimes it's not—proceed either way. Melt the butter in a medium ovenproof skillet—I like cast iron—over medium heat.

Whisk together the flour, cornmeal, sugar, baking powder, salt, and baking soda in a large bowl. Add the lemon-milk mixture, melted butter, and eggs and stir until evenly combined. Transfer the batter back to the skillet. Bake until golden and risen, 25 to 30 minutes.

BROWN BUTTER
When melting the butter, let it keep cooking until golden and nutty smelling. Proceed with the recipe as directed.

SCALLION
Add 1 bunch thinly sliced scallions to the melted butter. Proceed with the recipe as directed.

HONEY OR MAPLE
Substitute ¼ cup honey or maple syrup for the sugar. Proceed with the recipe as directed. Serve with butter and an extra drizzle of the same sweetener.

GARLIC & OIL BEANS

Active time: 5 minutes | Total time: 20 minutes | Serves 4

As I've mentioned, I make all of the recipes in this book in my real life. And I think I make these chickpeas most of all. Simmered in flavorful olive oil, they are so good and so easy and so flexible. Sometimes I make them with just the garlic, or just the shallot, or a bunch of scallions, because that's what I have. Sometimes I add a teaspoon of crushed red pepper flakes at the beginning, or stir in a handful of spinach at the end. I toss the finished beans with salad greens; I pile them on toast. I eat them over rice, under a dollop of yogurt, or alongside cottage cheese. I serve them as a vegetarian main with grilled vegetables, but they make a nice side for roasted or grilled lamb or chicken, too. See what I mean? Worth making all the time.

Two 15.5-ounce cans chickpeas or cannellini beans, drained and rinsed

½ cup olive oil

6 garlic cloves, smashed and peeled

1 shallot, halved and thinly sliced

3 to 4 sprigs fresh thyme or oregano, or ½ teaspoon dried

¾ teaspoon kosher salt

Freshly ground black pepper

Line a rimmed baking sheet with a layer of paper towels. Spread the chickpeas on the paper towels and shake the sheet around a bit to dry them off.

Combine the chickpeas, olive oil, garlic, shallot, herbs, salt, and several grinds of black pepper in a large skillet. Turn the heat to medium-high and cook, stirring occasionally, until the chickpeas are golden and beginning to blister, 10 to 15 minutes. Serve immediately and they will be slightly crispy, or let them cool in the oil and store in the fridge for about 5 days.

MAIN THINGS

Remember that old Rice Krispies treats commercial? A lady sits at the kitchen table reading a romance novel, a plate of finished treats stacked in front of her. "Mooom, are they ready yet?" a kid yells from the next room. "These things take time!" she hollers back before closing her novel, dusting her face with flour and fishbowl water, and slinking into the room to rave reviews.

These dinner recipes are kind of like that. No big effort, huge return. Alongside a vegetable, a starchy side, or both, these flexible main dishes come together fast and easy. Use the suggested Pantry+ Ingredients to dress them up, or play around with other flourishes from part 2. Standby for applause.

VEGGIE MAINS

PIZZA BROCCOLI

Active time: 35 minutes | Total time: 35 minutes | Serves 4

I don't know if this recipe came to me in a fever dream or a divine vision. All I know is one day I saw it, complete, and had to make it as soon as possible. It's a perfect pantry recipe: one fresh vegetable, plus a few of your go-to's, equals pizza vegetables. Sometimes I start it with a couple of crumbled sausages. Remove the sausage from the casings, cook until browned, then remove with a slotted spoon. The sausage drippings make a vegetable-forward dinner super satisfying if there happen to be staunch carnivores at the table. But it's pretty great sans pork. Serve with crusty bread or one of the dinner toasts on page 187.

6 tablespoons olive oil, divided

I onion (any color) or 2 shallots, thinly sliced

I teaspoon kosher salt, divided

Freshly ground black pepper

I bunch broccoli (about 3 crowns), trimmed and cut into long spears, or I head cauliflower, cut into large florets

One 28-ounce can whole peeled tomatoes, drained

¼ to ½ teaspoon crushed red pepper flakes, optional

8 ounces fresh mozzarella, torn into bite-size pieces

Fresh basil, torn, optional

Preheat oven to 450°F. Heat 2 tablespoons oil in a large ovenproof skillet over medium-high heat. Add onion, season with ¼ teaspoon salt and several grinds of black pepper and cook, stirring, until starting to darken at the edges, about 6 minutes. Transfer to a plate.

Add 2 tablespoons oil to the skillet and heat until shimmering. Add half the broccoli and cook, flipping once, until browned on two sides, about 4 minutes per side. Transfer to the plate with the onion as ready. Repeat with the remaining 2 tablespoons oil and broccoli. Season the vegetables with ½ teaspoon salt.

Return everything to the skillet and use your hands to crush the tomatoes over top. Season with remaining ¼ teaspoon salt, several grinds black pepper, and the crushed red pepper, if using. Top with mozzarella and transfer to the oven. Bake until the cheese is melted and the broccoli is just tender, 8 to 10 minutes. Heat the broiler.

Broil until the cheese is brown and bubbly, I to 2 minutes. Let cool slightly and top with basil, if using.

LENTIL
PARMESAN SOUP

Active time: 30 minutes | Total time: 1 hour | Serves 8

When it comes to canned and dried beans, I usually have both around. Before quarantine 2020, when hoarding beans became a collective obsession, lentils were my dried legume of choice. They're versatile and quick cooking in comparison to other dried bean varieties, and you can serve them to friends who claim to dislike beans with nary a complaint because they're lentils. That said, you can use a couple of cans of beans in place of the dried lentils in this soup or some of the Adaptable Beans (page 104). It's the base here—staple aromatics and a lot of tomato paste—that supports the variations, regardless of what you start with. The generous shower of Parmesan helps, too. If you taste it and you still want a little more zing, top with one of the flavored salts on page 56. It makes a lot and freezes great.

¼ cup olive oil, plus more for drizzling

2 yellow onions, chopped

2 carrots, chopped

2 celery stalks, chopped

4 garlic cloves, finely chopped

3 teaspoons kosher salt, divided

4 tablespoons tomato paste

2 cups dried brown or green lentils (soaked overnight if you remember)

1 dried bay leaf

8 cups water or vegetable broth

Parmesan rinds, optional

1 cup shredded or grated Parmesan, plus more for serving

Freshly ground black pepper, optional

Chopped cilantro or parsley leaves and stems, for serving

Heat the oil in a large heavy-bottom pot or Dutch oven over medium-high heat. Add the onions, carrots, celery, garlic, and 1 teaspoon salt and cook the vegetables, stirring often, until tender and beginning to brown, 10 to 12 minutes. Make a little hole in the middle of the vegetables so you can see the bottom of the pot and add the tomato paste. Cook, stirring it into the vegetables, until it starts to darken in color, about 2 minutes (really wait for it: once the tomato paste starts to caramelize it will add a *ton* of flavor to the soup, especially if you're using water and not broth). Stir in the lentils, bay leaf, water, Parmesan rinds, if using, and the remaining 2 teaspoons salt. Bring to a boil, reduce heat to simmer, and cook, stirring occasionally, until the lentils are tender, 30 to 35 minutes. (If you soaked the lentils they'll be done in about 15 minutes.)

Remove the soup from the heat and stir in the Parmesan. Taste and season with more salt and a few grinds of black pepper, if using.

Top the bowls with more shredded Parmesan (like a ¼ cup each), cilantro, and a drizzle of oil.

CHICKPEA CURRY

Active time: 30 minutes | Total time: 30 minutes | Serves 4

In 2001, when the Internet and my cooking abilities were still in their infancies, I found a recipe online for Easy Chana Dal. I can't say for sure, but my guess is I searched for "easy vegetarian recipes" or some such. I recall a photo of a faded recipe card, typed in Courier New with the ingredients and instructions for something close to the following recipe.

Chana Dal is the name for both a split chickpea (other dals include lentils or peas) as well as the soupy stew that results from cooking it with onions, tomatoes, and spices. Curry is a broad term that can refer to a sauce, a leaf, a powder, or a finished dish. The dish itself is found the world over from India and Thailand to Japan, South Africa, and Trinidad. This one is infused with spices often found in Indian curries like cumin, coriander, garlic, ginger, and turmeric with the addition of Western conveniences like ketchup: what that original recipe called for and what hooked me in the first place.

3 tablespoons vegetable oil or ghee

2 yellow onions, chopped

2 garlic cloves, chopped

2 tablespoons chopped fresh ginger

1½ teaspoons kosher salt

Freshly ground black pepper

4 teaspoon Curry Spice Blend (page 52) or curry powder

2 tablespoons ketchup or tomato paste

Two 15.5-ounce cans chickpeas, undrained

Steamed rice or Flatbreads (page 107) for serving

Yogurt, Zing! Sauce (page 82), cilantro, and Quickled onions (page 66) for serving, optional

Heat the oil in a large skillet over medium-high heat. Add the onions and cook, stirring occasionally until beginning to char around the edges, about 6 minutes. Add the garlic, ginger, salt, and several grinds of black pepper and cook, stirring, about 2 minutes. Add the spice blend and cook, stirring, until the mixture gets kind of sticky, about 1 minute. Add the ketchup and cook, stirring, about 1 minute.

Add the chickpeas and their liquid and stir to combine, scraping up any stuck-on spices from the bottom of the skillet. Bring to a simmer, reduce the heat, and cook, stirring occasionally, until slightly thickened, 8 to 10 minutes. Serve over rice or with flatbread, topped with yogurt, Zing! Sauce, cilantro, and pickled onions, if using.

> I've been cooking and riffing on this recipe for 20 years now. I've added fresh ginger, sometimes I stir in potatoes or spinach. I like canned chickpeas here, but try whatever beans you have around, canned or cooked from dried.

GREEN GALETTE

Active time: 10 minutes | Total time: 1 hour | Serves 4

One of my biggest tips when it comes to working with pie dough is don't rush the rolling. Trying to roll cold dough right out of the fridge is nearly impossible. You can do it, but the edges crack, it's hard to get an even thickness all the way across, and you can really work up a sweat. So before you preheat the oven, pull your dough out of the fridge and put it on the counter. By the time the oven's preheated, your dough should be at the perfect temperature to roll. This pie also works with pretty much any cooked vegetable you have around or tender summer veggies like cherry tomatoes or sliced zucchini. Serve with a salad and/or a fried egg on top.

All-purpose flour, for rolling

1 disk Go-To Pie Dough (page 111)

1 cup grated cheddar

2 cups Long-Cooked Greens (page 74)

1 egg, beaten

Preheat the oven to 350°F. On a lightly floured surface, roll the pie dough to about a 12-inch circle (don't worry about it being perfect; ovals and oblongs welcome here). Transfer the dough to a parchment-lined baking sheet.

Scatter ½ cup cheddar over the dough, leaving a 2-inch border. Top with the greens then the remaining ½ cup cheddar. Fold the edges of the dough over the filling, overlapping as necessary.

Brush the edges of the dough with the beaten egg. Bake until golden brown, 40 to 45 minutes. Let cool slightly before serving.

TOMATO AND CHEDDAR
Toss 2 cups halved cherry or grape tomatoes with 1 tablespoon olive oil, 1 teaspoon fresh thyme leaves (or ¼ teaspoon dried thyme), ¾ teaspoon kosher salt, and several grinds of black pepper. Use the tomatoes in place of the greens.

SQUASH AND MOZZ
Toss 2 cups thinly sliced butternut squash with 1 tablespoon olive oil, ¾ teaspoon kosher salt, several grinds of black pepper, and about 10 fresh sage leaves (if you have some). Use shredded mozzarella in place of the cheddar.

POTATO AND FETA
Toss 2 cups thinly sliced Yukon Gold potatoes (about 2 medium) with 1 tablespoon olive oil, 2 teaspoons fresh rosemary leaves, ¾ teaspoon kosher salt, and several grinds of black pepper. Use crumbled feta in place of the cheddar.

CHEATER'S TOMATO SOUP
(& A SPECIAL GRILLED CHEESE)

Active time: 10 minutes | Total time: 20 minutes | Serves 4

The base of this tomato soup is exactly the same as my easy marinara. Just add stock and you're on your way to a version that's way better than canned. You can certainly serve it with a regular grilled cheese, but a little layer of saucy flavor makes an old-fashioned sando feel like something new. Or just serve with toast.

4 cups 15-Minute Marinara (page 90)

4 cups Golden Chicken Stock (page 92)

Kosher salt

Freshly ground black pepper

8 slices bread

1 cup shredded cheddar or other nice melting cheese

¼ to ½ cup Flexo-Pesto (page 100), Slow-Roasted Tomatoes (page 79) or Zing! Sauce (page 82)

½ cup softened butter or mayonnaise

Combine the marinara and chicken stock in a large pot over medium heat. Cook, stirring occasionally, until the flavors meld (I know this is a lame indicator, but all it means is simmer for a bit until it's nice and warm and smells good), about 15 minutes; season with salt and a few grinds of black pepper. Keep warm over low heat.

Build the sandwiches with cheese and pesto, or whichever sauce you prefer. Heat a griddle or large skillet over medium heat. Spread both sides of the sandwiches with butter and cook, flipping halfway through, until the bread is golden brown and the cheese is melted, about 3 minutes per side.

Serve the sandwiches with the soup.

> Leftover rice, potatoes, or even stale bread can be blended into the soup for luscious creamy texture.

KRAUT
QUESADILLA

Active time: 5 minutes | Total time: 5 minutes | Serves 2 to 4

I was walking to the playground with my friend Justine and our kids one day when she casually mentioned they'd had kraut quesadillas for lunch. I think I tripped over the stroller I was pushing. What genius was this? All the melty cheese goodness of a quesadilla—with the probiotic benefits of fermented cabbage? I bet I can sneak it in and my daughter would never notice, I thought. Count me in! The kraut ques went on regular rotation in our house soon thereafter. Until Baby Girl discovered there was more than cheese sandwiched between her tortillas. If your kids will eat them, great. If not, more for you.

I tablespoon olive or vegetable oil

2 large (burrito-size) flour tortillas

I cup grated sharp cheddar cheese

I cup drained sauerkraut or kimchi, chopped

Heat the oil in a large skillet over medium-high heat. Add I tortilla and sprinkle with ½ cup cheese and ½ cup sauerkraut. Cook, undisturbed, until the cheese is melted and the tortilla is golden brown, about I minute. Fold one side of the tortilla over to close and transfer to a plate. Repeat with the remaining tortilla, cheese, and sauerkraut.

Sauerkraut is great here, but I also like it Roy Choi style: The pioneering Korean-American chef tucks kimchi inside his famous Kogi BBQ food truck's quesadillas. Also a good idea on a grilled cheese.

CHICKEN MAINS

GINGERY CHICKEN & RICE CHICKEN SOUP

Active time: 20 minutes | Total time: 45 minutes | Serves 4

I wish someone would make this soup for me when I get a cold. It's a grown-up version of my childhood favorite, Campbell's Chicken with Rice. I could hand over the recipe and supervise from a supine position (not that I am a kitchen micromanager or anything). It's warming with garlic and ginger and fortified with celery and shallots. Use whatever onion-type thing you have on hand—a whole red or yellow onion in place of the shallots, a bunch of scallions, or a couple of sliced leeks. No celery? Use carrots or fennel. No rice? Use tiny pasta or broken-up spaghetti. It's endlessly forgiving, just like I hope you'll be with me the next time I'm sick.

4 tablespoons vegetable or other neutral oil, divided

1 pound boneless, skinless chicken breasts or thighs

2 teaspoons kosher salt

Freshly ground black pepper

4 celery stalks, sliced, plus leaves for serving

4 garlic cloves, smashed and sliced

2-inch piece fresh ginger, peeled and chopped (about 2 tablespoons)

2 shallots, peeled and thinly sliced crosswise into rings

6 cups Golden Chicken Stock (page 92) or water

⅓ cup white rice (any kind)

1 tablespoon soy sauce or tamari

1 teaspoon rice vinegar

Quick Chili Oil (page 70) or hot sauce, for serving

Heat 2 tablespoons of oil in a large heavy-bottom pot over medium-high heat until shimmering. Season the chicken with 1 teaspoon salt and several grinds of black pepper. Add to the pot and cook, flipping once, until golden brown on both sides, 6 to 8 minutes; transfer the chicken to a plate.

Add the remaining 2 tablespoons of oil to the pot. Add the celery, garlic, ginger, and shallots to the pot and cook, stirring often, until softened, 3 to 4 minutes. Season with the remaining 1 teaspoon salt and several grinds of black pepper. Return the chicken to the pot and add the stock. Bring to a boil, reduce the heat, and simmer until the chicken is cooked through, 10 to 12 minutes. Transfer the chicken to a cutting board.

Add the rice to pot and simmer until tender, about 15 minutes. While the rice cooks, shred the chicken into bite-size pieces using two forks.

Return the chicken to pot and stir, giving it a minute to warm through. Stir in the soy sauce and vinegar. Serve topped with celery leaves and a drizzle of chili oil

217

SPICY LEMON CHICKEN SALAD

Active time: 30 minutes | Total time: 30 minutes | Serves 4

This recipe employs a technique called the postmarinade. I don't know if that's an official cooking term, but consider it official now. I learned it from my friend Theo, an amazing cook, who learned it from her parents, who emigrated from Corfu in the seventies. Theo's dad used a mixture of lemon juice, olive oil, water, and oregano, called "salamoura." He applied it to meat after grilling, to prevent flames from flaring up when cooking—common when oily marinades drip onto hot coals. Theo remembers her dad dipping everything in it, even hot dogs and hamburgers.

Since this marinade never touches raw meat, you really can use it on everything without wasting a drop. Plus it adds big, bright, herbaceous flavor at the last minute. No planning required. In this case, the pan juices from the chicken marry with the marinade to create a dressing that evenly coats the lettuce and is satisfyingly soaked up by the croutons.

1½ pounds chicken cutlets

Kosher salt

Freshly ground black pepper

I tablespoon olive oil

½ cup Garlicky Lemon Dressing (page 60), divided

½ cup grated Parmesan or pecorino cheese, divided

I head romaine, chopped or torn into bite-size pieces

I cup Oil and Herb Croutons (page 46)

Season the chicken with salt and a few grinds of black pepper. Heat the oil in a large skillet over medium-high heat. Add the chicken and cook, turning occasionally, until golden brown and cooked through, 7 to 12 minutes, depending on thickness. Remove the skillet from the heat and add ¼ cup dressing; turn the chicken to coat and set aside to marinate.

In a large bowl, mix the remaining ¼ cup dressing with ¼ cup Parmesan. Add the romaine and toss to coat. Slice the chicken, add to the bowl, and toss to combine. Serve topped with the croutons and remaining ¼ cup Parmesan.

SLOW-ROASTED
CHICKEN & POTATOES

Active time: 10 minutes | Total time: 3 hours 20 minutes | Serves 4

I have roasted hundreds of chickens in my lifetime. I've cooked them hot and fast, spatchcocked, and in pieces. Breast-side down and breast-side up; in cast-iron skillets, in a roasting pan, two at a time, side by side. I can say with confidence that there is no easier, more foolproof way to roast a chicken than low and slow. Especially for beginners. What results is close to a rotisserie chicken, with falling-off-the-bone tender meat. It takes a few hours, but you can basically set it and forget it. Use one of the spice blends on page 52 to dress it up if you like, but it'll be great with just salt and pepper.

2 pounds potatoes, any size, quartered

1 large onion, cut into eight 1-inch wedges

3 tablespoons olive oil, divided

1 tablespoon plus ½ teaspoon kosher salt, plus more

Freshly ground black pepper

One 3½- to 4-pound chicken

1 tablespoon Za'atar Blend, Curry Spice Blend, or Chili Powder Blend (page 52), optional

½ lemon and small handful fresh herbs, such as thyme, rosemary, or parsley, optional

> **Feeding a crowd? Add another chicken to the baking sheet and you'll be good to go.**

Preheat the oven to 300°F. On a rimmed baking sheet, toss the potatoes and onion with 2 tablespoons oil, ½ teaspoon salt, and several grinds of black pepper.

Pat the chicken dry with paper towels. Place on the baking sheet (scoot the potatoes and onion toward the edges to make room). Rub the chicken all over with the remaining 1 tablespoon oil, season inside and out with 1 tablespoon salt and about forty grinds of black pepper. Sprinkle with the spice mix, if using, and stuff the lemon and herbs, if using, inside the cavity.

Place the chicken breast-side up on the baking sheet and roast for 1 hour. Carefully add 1½ cups water to the baking sheet, gently shaking to distribute the liquid. Continue to roast, basting when you remember (aim for three times) until the chicken is golden brown and pull-apart tender, 1½ to 2 hours more. Let the chicken rest 10 to 15 minutes before carving or just pulling it apart. Serve with the onion and potatoes and be sure to use a spatula to scrape all the juicy business from the baking sheet.

PAN-ROASTED CHICKEN THIGHS
WITH FARRO, SHALLOTS & BAY LEAVES

Active time: 20 minutes | Total time: 50 minutes | Serves 4

Chicken thighs are one of the most forgiving parts you can make. You can forget about them for 20 minutes in the oven and they still come out pretty delicious. Truthfully, the chicken will be done before the farro is in this recipe, but because it finishes cooking in a flavorful broth, the meat stays juicy and tender while the skin crisps to golden perfection. This is truly one of my favorites in this book.

8 bone-in, skin-on chicken thighs (about 2½ pounds)

2 teaspoons kosher salt

Freshly ground black pepper

1 tablespoon olive oil

4 shallots, peeled and quartered lengthwise, or 2 red onions, cut into 1-inch wedges

1¼ cups farro

3 cups Golden Chicken Stock (page 92), chicken broth, or water

2 dried bay leaves

Preheat the oven to 425°F. Pat the chicken thighs dry with a paper towel and season all over with 2 teaspoons salt and several grinds of black pepper.

Heat the oil in a large 12-inch skillet over medium-high heat. Add the chicken, skin-side down, and cook, flipping halfway through, until golden brown on both sides, about 5 minutes per side. Transfer the chicken to a plate.

Add the shallots to the skillet and cook, stirring, about 1 minute, until transluscent. Add the farro and stir to combine. Add the chicken stock and bay leaves and bring to a simmer, scraping up any browned bits from the bottom of the pan. Once the broth has come to a simmer, return the chicken to the skillet, skin-side up. Carefully transfer to the oven and roast until the farro is tender and the chicken skin is crisp, 30 minutes.

CRISPY-FRIED CHICKEN CUTLETS

Active time: 30 minutes | Total time: 30 minutes | Serves 4

Few food items are as universally appealing as a crispy chicken cutlet. Stick them in a sandwich, smother them with cheese, or stand over the cutting board slicing them into thin strips and eating them before the kids notice. My favorite thing about these cutlets is that they can be coated in just about anything you can crush into tiny pieces: crackers, matzo, nuts or coarse nut flour, tortilla chips, unsweetened shredded coconut, or cereal. Add a couple of tablespoons of sesame seeds to the mix for extra credit. All cook up with unique flavor and crunch with the same easy technique. And, yes, it works for any type of cutlet. Try pounded boneless pork chops or thin fish filets; even thinly sliced extra-firm tofu can take it.

3 large eggs, beaten

Kosher salt

Freshly ground black pepper

2 cups panko, cracker crumbs, crushed cornflakes, unsweetened coconut, ground nuts, or coarse nut flour

4 boneless, skinless chicken breasts (about 2 pounds), split lengthwise

Vegetable oil, for frying

Place the eggs in a shallow baking dish; season with salt and several grinds of black pepper. Place the panko in a separate shallow baking dish and season with salt and several grinds of black pepper.

Season the chicken all over with salt and several grinds of black pepper. Working with one cutlet at a time, dip into the egg and turn to coat, letting excess egg drip back into the dish. Transfer to the panko and turn to coat, pressing to help the crumbs adhere. Transfer to a large plate or baking sheet.

Set a wire rack over a rimmed baking sheet. Heat about ½ inch of oil in a large skillet over medium heat. Drop a pinch of panko into the oil to check the temperature; it should sizzle quickly when it hits the oil. Working in batches, add the cutlets to the oil and cook, turning once, until golden brown and cooked through, 3 to 4 minutes per side; transfer to the rack. Repeat with the remaining cutlets, adding a little oil if necessary to keep it at ½-inch depth.

Cutlets can be cooked, cooled, and frozen for up to 3 months. Reheat in a 350°F oven until warm, 10 to 15 minutes.

SOME MORE IDEAS FOR CUTLETS

- Serve them as is with a green salad and a squeeze of lemon.

- Top with the Celery Salad with Cheese, Fruit, and Nuts (page 172).

- Sandwich in a soft bun with mayonnaise and chopped Quickles (page 66).

- Try them atop steamed white rice with chopped cucumbers, a splash of vinegar, and barbecue sauce doctored with a bit of soy sauce.

- Shave an apple and a head of fennel, toss with the fronds, lemon juice, olive oil, salt, and pepper. Pile on top for crunch on crunch.

- Layer with a spoonful of marinara (page 90), a slice of mozzarella, and a shower of Parmesan; broil until melted and bubbly. Side of spaghetti optional.

- Cut into strips and serve with one of the Creamy Dressings (page 62).

PASTA AND NEATBALLS

Active time: 10 minutes | Total time: 20 minutes | Serves 4 to 6

A quick reminder that if you come to class prepared, you get an A+ in spaghetti and meatballs. Stock that freezer, friends.

1 pound pasta, any shape

12 Oven-Baked Neatballs (page 96)

4 cups 15-Minute Marinara (page 90)

Parmesan or pecorino, grated, for serving

> Whenever possible, I serve stuff family style, straight from the cooking vessel. Just be sure to put down a trivet and cover hot handles with a dish towel.

Cook the pasta in a large pot of boiling salted water according to package directions for al dente.

Meanwhile, combine the neatballs and marinara in a large skillet over medium heat. Bring to a simmer and cook, stirring occasionally, until the neatballs are heated through, about 10 minutes.

Using a slotted spoon, transfer the neatballs to a bowl or platter. Using tongs, transfer the pasta directly to the skillet along with 1 cup pasta water. Increase the heat to high and cook, tossing, until the sauce thickens and coats the pasta, about 3 minutes. Serve the saucy pasta topped with neatballs and grated cheese.

WINTER PASTA
WITH GARLIC, OLIVES & LEMON

Active time: 25 minutes | Total time: 25 minutes | Serves 4

For thirteen years I lived in New York, where winter can be long and cold and dark and drive a person to consider one-way tickets to balmy island locales or self-medicate with huge bowls of noodles. Anecdotal evidence suggests that this pasta can shorten the duration and decrease severity of a common case of the Februaries. It's fast, warm, and bright, and since it's made solely with pantry ingredients, requires only slightly more effort than unfolding a beach chair. Lemon adds a bit of sunshine. Olives and Parmesan transport you to Sicily. A handful of long-lasting parsley reminds me that warmer weather will, in fact, come again.

1 pound pasta, any shape

Kosher salt

¼ cup olive oil

2 yellow onions, halved and thinly sliced

8 garlic cloves, smashed and sliced

Freshly ground black pepper

½ cup pitted and chopped Castelvetrano olives

½ cup chopped fresh herbs such as parsley, chives, basil, and/or mint

Juice of ½ lemon

Grated Parmesan, for serving

You can even add a can of drained tuna or some chopped sardines to this one.

Cook the pasta in a large pot of boiling salted water according to package directions for al dente.

Meanwhile, heat the oil in a large skillet over high heat. Add the onions and garlic and cook, tossing occasionally, until beginning to brown and blister, 3 to 4 minutes. Season with 1 teaspoon salt and several grinds of black pepper and continue to cook, tossing, until mostly dark brown all over, 6 to 8 minutes more. Reduce the heat as low as it will go while the pasta finishes cooking.

Using tongs, transfer the pasta directly from the pasta pot to the skillet along with 1 cup pasta water. Increase the heat to high and cook, tossing, until the liquid thickens and coats the pasta, about 3 minutes. Remove from the heat, add the olives, herbs, and lemon juice and toss to combine. Taste and season with more salt and a few grinds of black pepper if you like. Serve topped with the Parmesan.

228

WHATEVER VEGGIE IS IN THE PANTRY PASTA WITH SAUSAGE & ROASTED GARLIC

Active Time: 15 minutes | Total time: 45 minutes | Serves 4

You can make this recipe with pretty much any roasted vegetable. The sausage is the anchor here and plays nicely with most vegetable friends. Try it with eggplant or zucchini in August, or roasted butternut squash in the fall. Roasted onions are a good dead-of-winter option, and come spring, when all the leafy green things are sprouting through the wet earth, skip the roasting and just toss them in with the sausage until wilted and tender.

I large eggplant (about I pound), zucchini, peeled butternut squash, broccoli or cauliflower florets, or onions cut into bite-size pieces, or I pound spinach

8 tablespoons olive oil, divided

¾ teaspoon kosher salt

Freshly ground black pepper

I head garlic, halved crosswise

12 ounces pasta shape of your choosing

2 links Italian sausage (sweet or hot is OK), casings removed

¾ cup grated Parmesan, plus more for serving

½ cup chopped fresh parsley, basil, or mint leaves, for serving

Preheat the oven to 425°F. Toss the eggplant with 6 tablespoons of oil on a rimmed baking sheet. Season with ½ teaspoon salt and several grinds of black pepper. Shake to arrange in a single layer. Place the garlic on a square of foil; drizzle with I tablespoon oil and season with ¼ teaspoon salt and a few grinds of black pepper. Wrap the garlic and place on the baking sheet with the eggplant. Roast, tossing halfway through, until the eggplant is tender and brown and the garlic cloves are soft (unwrap to check—be careful of the steam), about 30 minutes. Squeeze the garlic cloves into the eggplant and discard the papery skins. (You can do this several hours ahead. I just leave mine on the stovetop until it's time to eat.)

Meanwhile, cook the pasta according to package directions for al dente. Drain and reserve I cup pasta water.

While the pasta cooks, heat the remaining I tablespoon oil in a large skillet over medium-high heat until shimmering. Add the sausage and cook, breaking up with a wooden spoon, until cooked through and dark brown in spots, about 5 minutes. Add the roasted eggplant and garlic and cook, tossing, for I minute. Add the pasta and the reserved pasta water and cook, tossing (liquid should be bubbling vigorously) until the liquid thickens and coats the pasta, about 2 minutes. Remove from heat, add the Parmesan and parsley, and toss to combine. Serve with more Parmesan.

MISO RAMEN WITH
MUSHROOMS & GREENS

Active time: 30 minutes | Total time: 30 minutes | Serves 4

When one is very hungry and very cold, there is nothing quite like a bowl of ramen to satisfy your belly and warm you up from the inside out. There are three primary types of Ramen. From lightest to richest they are shio (salt), shoyu (soy), and miso (umami) plus a fourth, tonkatsu, which refers to one made with a pork stock. This one features pantry superstar miso paste, which adds body and rich umami flavor to the chicken broth base. Other pantry MVPs, soy sauce and rice vinegar, help balance the broth. Curly ramen noodles are my first choice here but the soup will still be delicious with whatever long noodles you have. Just be careful when slurping.

6 ounces dried ramen noodles, or 8 ounces soba, udon, rice noodles, or spaghetti

2 tablespoons vegetable oil

4 garlic cloves, chopped

1½-inch piece fresh ginger, peeled and chopped

12 ounces cremini and/or shiitake mushrooms, tough stems removed, sliced

6 cups Golden Chicken Stock (page 92) or water

2 tablespoons soy sauce or tamari

2 tablespoons rice vinegar

1 teaspoon sugar

1 bunch mustard greens, kale, or spinach, tough ends trimmed (about 4 cups)

4 tablespoons yellow miso paste

4 jammy-yolk eggs (page 149)

Quick Chili Oil (page 70) or crushed red pepper flakes, for serving, optional

Cook the ramen noodles according to package directions (usually about 4 to 6 minutes). Drain the noodles in a colander and rinse under cold water to cool; drain again and set aside.

Heat the oil in a large pot over medium-high heat. Add the garlic and ginger and cook, stirring, until fragrant, about 30 seconds. Add the mushrooms and cook, stirring often until brown and softened, 6 to 8 minutes. Add the stock, soy sauce, vinegar, and sugar and bring to a simmer. Add mustard greens and stir until wilted, 2 to 4 minutes. Remove from heat.

Transfer ¼ cup of the broth to a small bowl; whisk in the miso then stir the mixture back into the pot.

Peel the eggs and cut each in half. Divide the soup among 4 bowls. Top with 1 egg and chili oil, if using.

FREESTYLE BAKED PASTA

Active time: 30 minutes | Total Time: 45 minutes | Serves 4 to 6

This dish was inspired by one of my favorite things I've ever eaten in my whole life: the baked rigatoni at Sabotino's in Baltimore City's Little Italy. It combines béchamel with marinara to create an irresistible bubbling dish of creamy, tomatoey pasta. The cool thing about this version is that if you stick to the ratios of pasta to sauce, you can create endless variations on the theme. Substitute a cup of the marinara for some pesto (page 100) or double the béchamel and skip the marinara entirely for a very special mac and cheese. Leave the vegetables out or double down, depending on if you're feeling virtuous or if you need to make room in your crisper drawer. It's very adaptable—make it your own.

2 tablespoons unsalted butter

2 tablespoons all-purpose flour

2 cups whole milk

Kosher salt

Freshly ground black pepper

2½ cups grated Parmesan, divided

I pound short pasta, such as ziti, rigatoni, penne, or fusilli

4 cups 15-Minute Marinara (page 90), or your favorite jarred sauce

2 cups Long-Cooked Greens (page 74) or leftover roasted vegetables (page 73), optional

I pound mozzarella (preferably fresh), torn or cut into bite-size pieces

Preheat the oven to 350°F. Lightly oil a 3-quart baking pan (9-by-13-inch or similar). Bring a large pot of water to a boil.

Melt the butter in a medium pot over medium heat. Add the flour and cook, stirring constantly with a wooden spoon or spatula, until smooth, I to 2 minutes. Gradually add the milk, in about four additions, whisking after each. Bring to a simmer, whisking occasionally. Continue to cook, whisking often, until the mixture thickens and coats the back of a spoon, 6 to 8 minutes. Remove from the heat and add ½ teaspoon salt, several grinds of black pepper, and 2 cups Parmesan, whisking until smooth. Set aside.

Season the boiling water generously with salt. Add the pasta and cook 5 minutes (it'll continue to cook in the oven so don't worry that it's not tender yet); drain and transfer to a large bowl.

To the pasta, add the Parmesan sauce, the marinara, greens, and half the mozzarella. Fold gently a few times to coat the pasta, but it should still look streaky. Transfer to the prepared baking dish. Top with the remaining mozzarella and Parmesan.

Bake until bubbling, about 15 minutes. Set the oven to broil and broil until the cheese starts to brown in spots, I or 2 minutes. Let cool slightly before serving.

PASTA WITH
ZUCCHINI, NUTS & HERBS

Active time: 30 minutes | Total time: 30 minutes | Serves 4

Before you get mad about using only twelve ounces of pasta here, know that it's really plenty alongside a pound and a half of vegetables. Plus, it's nice to have a little bit of uncooked pasta around so you can toss it into soups or make a single serving of pasta with butter and cheese "for the kids." Try it with zucchini or summer squash, but it works with bite-size broccoli or cauliflower florets, too.

Kosher salt

½ cup olive oil

½ cup chopped pecans or walnuts

2 garlic cloves, thinly sliced

1½ pounds zucchini or other summer squash (about 3 medium), thinly sliced (about 6 cups)

Freshly ground black pepper

12 ounces pasta shape of choice

Zest and juice of ½ lemon (about ½ teaspoon and 1 tablespoon respectively)

½ cup grated Parmesan or pecorino

1 cup fresh basil, mint, or parsley leaves, for serving

This one is excellent cold out of the fridge: Pasta salad, but better.

Bring a large pot of salted water to a boil.

Combine the oil, pecans, and garlic in your largest skillet (ideally 12 inches) and place over medium heat. Cook, stirring, until the nuts and garlic are toasted, 2 to 5 minutes, depending on the strength of your stove. Using a slotted spoon, transfer the nuts and garlic to a small bowl.

Increase the heat to medium high. Add the zucchini to the oil in the skillet and toss to coat. Season with 1 teaspoon salt and several grinds of black pepper and cook, tossing occasionally until the zucchini is very tender and at least half is deeply golden brown (it's a lot of squash; not every piece will take on a ton of color), 12 to 15 minutes.

Meanwhile, cook the pasta according to package directions for al dente; reserve ½ cup pasta water and drain. Add the pasta and pasta water to the zucchini and cook, tossing, until the liquid is reduced and coats the pasta, about 30 seconds. Add the lemon zest and juice, half the nut and garlic mixture, ¼ cup Parmesan, and ½ cup basil leaves and toss to combine.

Serve topped with the remaining ¼ cup Parmesan, nut and garlic mixture, and ½ cup basil leaves.

SEAFOOD MAINS
CLAMS & BEANS WITH ZING! SAUCE

Active time: 20 minutes | Total time: 20 minutes | Serves 4

Clams are one of the things I love to cook maybe more than I love to eat. Watching them open one by one is truly one of my favorite cooking tasks. Eat these clams alone or ladled over thick toasted country bread. On another night, try a cup of slow-roasted tomatoes in place of the Zing! Sauce—that rendition is especially good tossed with pasta.

3 tablespoons olive oil, plus more for serving.

1 large shallot (or 2 small), finely chopped

3 garlic cloves, chopped

½ cup water

36 littleneck clams or mussels or a mix, washed

2 cans butter beans or cannellini beans, drained and rinsed

⅓ cup Zing! Sauce (page 82) or Flexo-Pesto (page 100)

4 thick slices country bread, toasted

Heat the oil in a large pot over medium-high heat. Add the shallot and garlic and cook, stirring until fragrant, about 1 minute. Add the water and clams and bring to a simmer. Cover the pot, reduce the heat to medium, and cook, covered, peeking now and then. Using tongs or a slotted spoon transfer the clams to a bowl as they open (discard any that stay closed), 6 to 10 minutes.

Add the beans to the pot and cook, stirring, until warmed through, 1 to 2 minutes. Return the clams to the pot and stir in the Zing! Sauce.

Drizzle the toast with oil and ladle the clams, beans, and broth over top. Serve with a knife and fork.

SHRIMP & CHORIZO WITH CRUSHED CROUTONS

Active time: 15 minutes | Total time: 15 minutes | Serves 4

Dried chorizo adds big flavor to this fifteen-minute meal. It's packed with garlic and paprika and renders stunning—calling Bob Ross fans—burnt sienna–colored oil in which you cook the shrimp. Toss with more garlic, parsley, and some crushed croutons (though a handful of salty cracker crumbs would work, too), and dinner's done.

4 tablespoons olive oil

4 ounces dried chorizo, sliced

4 garlic cloves, chopped

1½ pounds large shrimp, peeled and deveined

1 tablespoon fresh lemon juice or vinegar

Kosher salt

Freshly ground black pepper

½ cup chopped fresh parsley

½ cup crushed Oil and Herb Croutons (page 46)

Heat 2 tablespoons oil in a large skillet over medium-high heat. Add half the chorizo, garlic, and shrimp and cook, turning halfway through, until the shrimp are just cooked through, 3 to 4 minutes. Transfer to a plate and repeat with the remaining oil, chorizo, garlic, and shrimp. Return everything to the skillet and toss to combine. Remove from the heat, add the lemon juice, and season with salt and a few grinds of black pepper. Add the parsley and croutons and toss to combine. Serve straight from the skillet.

> The chorizo and croutons make this super savory. To balance things out, serve with a big pile of lightly dressed salad greens.

SIMMERED FISH WITH TOMATOES & BACON

Active time: 30 minutes | Total time: 40 minutes | Serves 4

Fish can be a little intimidating to cook. It can stick to the pan, it's easy to overcook, and it can make the whole house smell like the boardwalk after a storm surge. But I've figured out ways to cook fish so those things don't happen. Cooked gently in bacon-flavored tomatoes, most types of fish turn out moist and tender every time. And, unlike searing fish on the stovetop, you won't need to boil a pot of vinegar to cover the smell afterward. Serve this one over toast or rice, with a crunchy salad on the side.

4 slices bacon

I red onion, halved and thinly sliced

Kosher salt

Freshly ground black pepper

½ teaspoon crushed red pepper flakes, optional

One 28-ounce can whole peeled tomatoes

1½ pounds firm white fish, such as halibut, cod, or pollock

Olive oil for drizzling

Chopped fresh chives or parsley, for serving

Cook the bacon in a large skillet over medium heat, turning occasionally, until crisp, 5 to 7 minutes. Transfer to a plate.

Increase the heat to medium high. To the drippings in skillet, add the onion and season with ½ teaspoon salt and several grinds of black pepper. Cook, stirring occasionally, until the onion starts to brown, about 4 minutes. Add the crushed red pepper flakes, if using, and the tomatoes, breaking up with your hands or a spatula to bite-size pieces; season with ½ teaspoon salt and more black pepper. Bring to a simmer.

Season the fish all over with salt and pepper and nestle in the sauce. Drizzle with oil and cover the skillet. Reduce the heat to low and cook, covered, until the fish is just cooked through, 3 to 5 minutes depending on thickness.

Uncover, top with chives, and crumble bacon over top.

SPICED SHEET PAN SALMON WITH LEMON & CHICKPEAS

Active time: 15 minutes | Total time: 30 minutes | Serves 4

I don't love salmon. Phew, I said it. But most people love it, and I really don't want to "yuck anyone's yum." So I keep frozen fillets in the freezer and am committed to finding ways to prepare it so everybody likes it. The key for me is to add (read: distract with) other big flavors. Caramelized lemon and onions and an assertive spice blend do the trick here. I like it a lot with the Curry Spice Blend, but it tastes great with any of the spice blends on page 52. Or, if you don't need distracting, salt and pepper.

Two 15.5-ounce cans chickpeas, drained, rinsed, and patted dry

1 yellow onion, halved and thinly sliced

1 lemon, thinly sliced crosswise

¼ cup plus 1 teaspoon olive oil

1½ teaspoons kosher salt, divided

½ teaspoon freshly ground black pepper, divided

1½-pound-piece salmon

1 teaspoon Curry Spice Blend (page 52) or curry powder

Heat the broiler to high with the oven rack in the highest position. Toss the chickpeas, onion, and lemon with ¼ cup oil, ¾ teaspoon salt, and ¼ teaspoon black pepper on a rimmed baking sheet. Broil, shaking the baking sheet halfway through, until the onion starts to brown, 5 to 8 minutes.

Meanwhile, rub the salmon with the 1 teaspoon oil, the spice blend, and remaining ¾ teaspoon salt and ¼ teaspoon black pepper. Remove the baking sheet from the oven and lower the oven temperature to 300°F. Scoot the chickpeas, onion, and lemon toward the edges of the baking sheet and place the salmon in the center. Return to the oven on the center rack and bake until the salmon is opaque and just cooked through, 15 to 20 minutes.

MEAT MAINS

BRAISED BEEF
WITH TOMATOES & ONIONS

Active time: 30 minutes | Total Time: 3 hours | Serves 6

Once you learn the mechanics of a basic braise, you'll be hooked on the meltingly tender results. I offer you here a super straightforward formula that can be adapted with lots of different flavors, depending on the state of your mood and/or pantry. Eat it as is, over or alongside something that will soak up the sauce, like crusty bread, crushed boiled potatoes, or rice. Or shred the meat, stir it through the tomato base, and toss it with pasta and Parmesan. Tuck it into tortillas or inside a toasted roll. No matter where you take it, it makes a lot and freezes great.

2 to 3 pounds boneless chuck roast or boneless short ribs, cut into 3- to 4-inch pieces

2½ teaspoons kosher salt

Freshly ground black pepper

2 tablespoons olive oil

4 onions (any kind), quartered and peeled

1 head garlic, halved

Several sprigs fresh herbs, whatever you have on hand

One 28-ounce can whole peeled tomatoes

Preheat the oven to 350°F. Season the beef all over with the salt and a few grinds of black pepper. Heat the oil in a large, heavy-bottom pot or Dutch oven over medium-high heat. Add the beef and brown on all sides, 8 to 10 minutes (reduce the heat to medium if the bottom of the pot starts to get really dark). Transfer to a plate.

Add the onions, garlic, and herbs to the pot. Cook, stirring often, until the onions and garlic begin to brown, about 5 minutes. Add the tomatoes and their juices, crushing with your hands as you add them, and about half a can of water and stir to combine, scraping up any browned bits from the bottom of the pot.

Return the meat to the pot, nestling it in the onions and spooning some of the tomatoes and herbs on top. Return to a simmer over medium-high heat and cover. Transfer to the oven and cook, turning the meat halfway through, until it's super tender, about 2 hours. Remove the meat from the pot and slice or shred. Alternately, let the meat cool in the sauce. The meat can be braised up to 4 days ahead of time. Reheat in the sauce.

CRISPY SPICED LAMB
WITH TAHINI & YOGURT

Active time: 30 minutes | Total time: 30 minutes | Serves 4

I once waited in line for an hour and a half for a spiced lamb pita. It was at Miznon, a famous little falafel and pita shop in Paris (now with locations around the world) and it was totally worth it. That was many moons ago. Now you can order their Lamb Kebab Kit on the Internet and have it shipped right to your door. Sigh. For a similar vibe, in both fewer minutes and minus tax and shipping, try this crispy lamb pita. Instead of forming the spiced lamb mixture around skewers and grilling, you'll crisp it up in a hot skillet then top everything with your own homemade Quickles and tahini sauce. Nothing compares to Miznon's warm pita but a Whole Wheat Cumin Flatbread is a tasty substitution.

I tablespoon olive oil

2 teaspoons cumin seeds, or 2 teaspoons ground cumin

I teaspoon coriander seeds, or 1¼ teaspoons ground coriander

4 garlic cloves, finely chopped

I pound ground lamb or beef

I teaspoon paprika

½ teaspoon cinnamon

I teaspoon kosher salt

Freshly ground black pepper

½ cup plain Greek yogurt

4 Whole Wheat Cumin Flatbreads (page I07), pita, flour tortillas, or naan, warmed

Quickled onions, cucumbers, and/or chilies (page 66), optional

Tahini Sauce (page 80), fresh cilantro and/or mint, for serving

Heat the oil in a medium (I0-inch) skillet over medium-high heat until shimmering. Add the cumin, coriander, and garlic and cook, stirring, until fragrant, about 30 seconds. Add the lamb, paprika, cinnamon, salt, and several grinds of black pepper. Cook, breaking up the lamb with a spatula, until no longer pink. Use the spatula to press the lamb mixture into an even layer across the skillet. Let cook, undisturbed, until crispy on the bottom, about 2 minutes. Use the spatula to turn the lamb, then press it into an even layer again; cook 2 more minutes. Turn, press, and cook undisturbed, until crispy in most spots, 2 more minutes.

Spread the yogurt on the flatbreads and season with salt and black pepper. Top with the lamb, pickles, tahini sauce, and herbs.

Works with ground beef as well. Also delicious over rice.

SHEET PAN SAUSAGE
WITH CABBAGE & PICKLED ONIONS

Active time: 10 minutes | Total time: 45 minutes | Serves 4

This is truly one of easiest, most satisfying weeknight dishes of all time. Plus it buys you about thirty minutes of hands-off time during which you can finish up that last email you were writing before you realized it was almost 7 p.m., walk the dog (if you're OK leaving the house with the oven on—I am), or just sit back and relax. Pickled onions are a tasty contrast to the sweetness of the roasted ones, but vinegar offers a similar tangy brightness if that's what you have ready to go.

1 head green or red cabbage, halved, cored, and cut into 1-inch wedges (about 1½ pounds)

1 red or yellow onion, halved and cut into ½-inch wedges

6 tablespoons olive oil

1 teaspoon kosher salt

Freshly ground black pepper

4 sweet or spicy Italian sausages

Quickled onions (page 66) or 1 tablespoon cider vinegar

Dijon mustard, for serving

Preheat the oven to 450°F. Toss together the cabbage, onion, and oil on a rimmed baking sheet. Season with the salt and several grinds of black pepper and nestle the sausages among the vegetables. Roast, shaking the baking sheet halfway through, until the cabbage is brown on the edges, 25 to 30 minutes. Turn the oven to broil and broil until the onions and sausages are browned, about 3 minutes more.

Scatter the pickled onions over everything and serve with Dijon mustard.

> You could also stuff all of this inside a split toasted roll.

ROASTED POTATO SALAD
WITH CHORIZO & ALMONDS

Active time: 10 minutes | Total time: 40 minutes | Serves 4

I don't make meat the main event every night. However, there are a couple of excitable meat eaters in my house (ages thirty-three and seventeen months). In an effort to avoid making a "side steak" all the time, I came up with this dinner salad. It has a little bit of everything: crunchy greens, tender sweet potatoes, salty cheese, and toasty nuts. And meat! I like the spice and heat from dried chorizo, but crisped-up salami from the deli could work, too. I've even used little pepperonis. Genius! Make it with sturdy greens that can take the heat: a little wilt is great, a lot is sad.

8 small sweet potatoes or Yukon Gold potatoes (about 2½ pounds), halved lengthwise

2 onions, any kind, halved lengthwise and cut into ½-inch wedges

4 tablespoons olive oil, plus more for almonds

Kosher salt

Freshly ground black pepper

4 ounces dried chorizo, salami, soppressata, or pepperoni, thinly sliced

⅓ cup toasted almonds, hazelnuts, or pistachios, chopped

I bunch kale or collard greens, tough stems removed and leaves torn

I shallot, thinly sliced

4 tablespoons Dijon Vinaigrette (page 60)

Shaved sharp cheddar or Parmesan, for serving

Preheat the oven to 400°F with racks in upper and lower thirds. Toss the sweet potatoes and onions with oil, I teaspoon salt, and several grinds of black pepper. Arrange on two rimmed baking sheets. Roast, rotating the baking sheets from top to bottom halfway through, until the potatoes are tender and golden brown on the underside, 25 to 30 minutes.

Flip the sweet potatoes cut-side up. Divide the chorizo between the baking sheets and continue to roast until the chorizo is tender and heated through, 3 to 5 minutes.

In a small bowl, toss the almonds with a little oil and season with salt and pepper. In another bowl, toss the kale and shallot with the vinaigrette and top with the sweet potatoes, roasted onions, chorizo, cheddar, and almonds.

WEEKNIGHT CASSOULET

Active time: 40 minutes | Total time: 40 minutes | Serves 4

I'm nervous to call this a "cassoulet," a dish that takes, oh, I don't know, three days to make. There's no duck, the beans are basic, and you don't have to order anything from France. And that's the point. You get a similar saucy bean experience, complete with irresistible bread crumb topping, without any advanced planning and in a fraction of the time. When I mentioned this to my husband, he was like, "I don't think the cassoulet council is going to come after you." If they do, I'll just feed them dinner.

4 tablespoons olive oil, divided

4 sweet Italian sausages
(about I pound)

I onion (any color), chopped

I celery stalk, thinly sliced

2 garlic cloves, smashed and
chopped

Kosher salt

Freshly ground black pepper

Two 15.5-ounce cans cannellini or
white northern beans

I cup water

I teaspoon white wine vinegar

I cup panko, coarse fresh bread
crumbs, or cracker crumbs

⅓ cup chopped fresh parsley

Heat 2 tablespoons oil in a medium skillet over medium-high heat. Prick the sausages all over with the tip of a knife. Add the sausages to the skillet and cook, turning occasionally, until brown all over, 5 to 7 minutes. Transfer to a cutting board.

Add the onion, celery, and garlic to the skillet and season with salt and a few grinds of black pepper. Cook, stirring often, until softened, about 5 minutes. Add the beans and their liquid, the water, and season with salt and a few grinds of black pepper. Bring to a simmer. Slice the sausages and return to the skillet. Stir in the vinegar and remove from heat.

Preheat the broiler with the rack in the top position. In a small bowl, combine the panko, parsley, and remaining 2 tablespoons oil. Season the bread crumbs with a little salt and a few grinds of black pepper and scatter over the beans and sausage. Transfer the skillet to the oven and broil (watch carefully! Broilers vary like crazy) until the top is golden brown, I to 2 minutes. Let cool slightly before serving.

AFTER THOUGHTS

When I was working in test kitchens, my comrades and I could each cook several dishes a day that served four or more. That equals upward of twenty servings of Thanksgiving dinner, brisket, or brownies available for eating at any hour of the workday. It's part of the job to taste and give feedback, but one can only try so many corn bread stuffings before noon.

I abhor food waste. Which meant there were always lots of leftovers to take home. Pantry cooking means using what you have on hand, including leftovers. But, truth be told, I'm not the biggest fan of leftovers. One: until two months ago, I didn't own a microwave, so reheating was harder than it ought to be. Two, and more to the point: most hot food is intended to be eaten right away, decreasing in value with every minute it sits, like a new car driven off the lot. (Save a few special examples like eggplant Parmesan, which is so wonderful both hot and cold the next day it needs no fussing.)

Leftovers need to be *made* over. Not remade from scratch, of course, just updated with some other items you likely have on hand. These recipes are my go-tos for using up different bits and pieces, especially at the end of the week before my next big shop. You and I won't have exactly the same leftovers around, but I've provided guidance here that I hope will cover the basics. Use the ingredients and the methods as a jump-off and let your pantry and leftovers be your guide.

SHEET PAN
TACOS

Active time: 10 minutes | Total time: 10 minutes | Servings vary

In her book My Mexico City Kitchen, *chef Gabriela Cámara says, "What makes tacos great is that you don't need a recipe to make one." She fills hers with stews, leftover mole, even soft-boiled eggs. The only taco rule, she says, is "that it be wrapped in a tortilla and eaten with your hands." Tacos are a smart way to use up little bits of tasty this and delicious that that may accumulate throughout a week of cooking. Building them on a sheet pan means you can make a lot at once. Everybody might not get the same taco, but that's part of the fun. Use whatever cooked protein or hearty vegetables you have on hand—meat, beans, tofu, or a quickly scrambled egg—add cheese and any toppings you like. Fold and eat.*

Tortillas

Cheddar cheese or another good melter

Leftover chopped or shredded cooked meat, roasted vegetables, beans, or tofu, or, if none apply, scrambled eggs, two per person

Hot sauce, salsa, cilantro, pickled onions, sliced fresh chilies, sliced avocado, etc., for serving

Preheat the broiler to high with a rack in the highest position. Arrange the tortillas in a single layer on a rimmed baking sheet. Broil until warm, about 1 minute. Remove the baking sheet from the oven and flip the tortillas over.

Top each tortilla with a little cheese and some leftovers. Return to the oven and broil until the cheese is melted and the fillings are heated through, 1 to 2 minutes.

Serve with your favorite taco toppings.

SPAGHETTI
PANCAKES

Active time: 15 minutes | Total time: 15 minutes | Servings vary

This is another way to stretch a not-quite serving-size portion of leftovers. It's also a clever way to use the same pasta with butter and cheese you served your kids for the last two days in a new way. The method works with pasta, mashed potatoes, or cooked rice. Top with more cheese and/or serve with a little marinara for dipping.

I egg for each cup leftovers

Leftover cooked pasta, rice, or grains

¼ cup grated Parmesan, pecorino, or cheddar cheese, plus more for serving

Kosher salt

Freshly ground black pepper

Olive oil or vegetable oil for cooking

Beat the egg into the leftovers along with the Parmesan; season with salt and a few grinds of black pepper. Heat a little oil in a large nonstick skillet over medium-high heat. Add the leftover mixture ¼ cup at a time and cook, flipping once, until golden brown on both sides, 2 to 3 minutes total. Transfer to a paper towel–lined plate to drain. Serve topped with more Parmesan.

This same method works with leftover mashed or lightly crushed potatoes, too.

OPEN-FACED
PATTY MELT

Active time: 15 minutes | Total time: 15 minutes | Serves 1 to 2

As soon as meat gets sliced, it can start to dry out—another reason it can be hard to love leftovers. But this patty melt saves even the driest slices from leftover rejection. The house sauce keeps everything nice and moist, as does the blanket of melted cheese. I suggest eating this slightly messy open-faced sandwich straight from the baking sheet in front of the TV, preferably after the kids go to bed (though they will probably like it, too). Unfold a dish towel on the coffee table and place the warm sheet pan on top. Sit cross-legged on the floor in front of it. Pour yourself a very nice glass of red wine. Serve with a knife and fork and a side of napkins.

2 pieces toasted crusty bread

¼ cup House Sauce (page 83)

Leftover meat, such as in Slow-Roasted Chicken and Potatoes (page 220), Braised Beef with Tomatoes and Onions (page 247), or Oven-Baked Neatballs (page 96), sliced or smashed

4 ounces sliced cheddar or other melting cheese

Kosher salt

Freshly ground black pepper

Heat the broiler to high with a rack in the highest position. Arrange the toast on a rimmed baking sheet. Divide the sauce between the toasts and top with your meat of choice and the cheddar. Broil until heated through and the cheddar is melted, about 2 minutes. Season with salt and a few grinds of black pepper.

OFFICE BOWLS

When I worked in an office, my building sat atop a very excellent food court. There were tacos and chopped salads, sushi and skinny pizza, dumplings and barbecue, and bagels to boot. Needless to say, I dropped some serious coin on lunch. More often than not, though, I went for an office bowl: a filling yet feel-good formula of grains, protein, and a couple of veg-heavy sides. And I wasn't the only one. Every day the line snaked all the way past the sandwich place and around cupcake corner, toward palm tree village, an improbable midmall greenhouse planted with sixteen Washingtonia robusta palms (I looked it up). We waited in that line, tapped on our phones, refreshing emails or Instagram, shuffling toward the register where we dropped, like, sixteen dollars on a glorified salad.

Those were the days!

But why pay all that money and wait in a boring queue when you can build your own office bowl with all you've learned to make in the previous pages? With a handful of things ready to go—leftover protein, washed greens, cooked grains—plus a dressing or a crunch, you can create a delicious, satisfying, portable lunch (or dinner) at a fraction of the cost.

You can now mix and match your staples and homemade favorites in infinite variations. Look at everything you made! Look at all you can do! Look at all of the money you saved. Tastes delicious, doesn't it?

These bowls require some assembly, but that's it. Start with a base of grains, rice, or greens and build from there. Here are a few of my favorite combos:

OFFICE BOWL 1
Grains + Lemon-Lime Cabbage (page 168) + roasted sweet potatoes + Adaptable Beans (page 104) + avocado + Sesame-Ginger Dressing (page 61)

OFFICE BOWL 2
Greens + cooked chicken + Creamy Caesar Dressing (page 46) + Oil and Herb Croutons (page 46)

OFFICE BOWL 3
Rice + Long-Ccooked Greens (page 74) + Frico-Fried Eggs (page 152) + Quick Chili Oil (page 70) or Flexo-Pesto (page 100)

OFFICE BOWL 4
Rice + Adaptable Beans (page 104) + Out-of-Season Salsa (page 82) or Zing! Sauce (page 82) + Cheese Crispies (page 46)

OFFICE BOWL 5
Grains + Garlic & Oil Beans (page 203) + Slow
Roasted Tomatoes (page 79)+ Olive and Herb
Dressing (page 61) + Sliced Mozzarella

OFFICE BOWL 6

Greens + hard cooked egg + Quickles
(page 66) + tuna + sliced radishes + lemon +
olive oil

OPPORTUNITY SOUP

Active time: 20 minutes | Total time: 30 minutes | Serves 6 to 8

One of my big goals of this section—and this book—is to encourage you to waste less: to use up and make delicious all of your groceries, to really make them work for you. But we can all get lazy, tossing out uneaten leftovers or the random odds and ends left in the crisper. According to the nonprofit Feeding America, seventy-two billion pounds of food is wasted every year, not including waste at home. We can do better. We must *do better.*

At the end of the week or before my next big shopping trip, I take stock of what I have on hand, primarily in the fridge, where I keep more perishable items, but also in the cupboard and freezer. Then I make this soup, and I hope you will, too. This soup is your chance to use up any lingering leftovers and forgotten vegetables and turn them into something delicious without a ton of effort. It's also a great way to do an inventory of your pantry so you don't buy in excess or double down on something you never got to the previous week (cabbage, stop hiding from me!). Half a random red onion? Start sautéing. A single sausage from a few nights ago? Slice and toss it in. Why would anyone save a quarter cup of orzo? This soup is why. You'll be left with a big, nourishing pot that's good for you, good for your wallet, and good for the planet. It tastes pretty good, too.

¼ cup olive oil

2 sausage links, casings removed, or a few slices of bacon, chopped

½ to 1 onion

1 to 2 carrots, chopped

1 to 2 celery stalks, chopped

2 garlic cloves, chopped

Kosher salt

Freshly ground black pepper

3 to 4 teaspoons dried spices or herbs such as ground cumin, dried oregano, or ground coriander

One 14-ounce can tomatoes (diced, crushed, or whole peeled smashed) or one 6-ounce can tomato paste

6 cups broth or water

1 bay leaf

OPTIONAL ADDITIONS

About ½ cup uncooked rice, farro, or tiny pasta (or broken-up big pasta)

A few handfuls (and up to a bunch) torn hearty greens or Long-Cooked Greens (page 74)

One 15.5-ounce can of beans, drained and rinsed

Flexo-Pesto (page 100), Zing! Sauce (page 82), Cheese Crispies (page 46), or Oil and Herb Croutons (page 46) for serving

(recipe continues on page 271)

OPPORTUNITY SOUP

Heat the oil in a large pot over medium high heat. Add the sausage and cook, stirring often, until browned and crisp, 5 to 7 minutes. Add the onion, carrot, celery, and garlic, season with salt and a few grinds of black pepper and cook until the vegetables start to soften, about 5 minutes.

Add the spices and cook, stirring until fragrant, about I minute. Add the tomatoes and cook until the bottom of the pot just starts to get sticky, about 2 minutes. Add the broth and bay leaf and season with salt and a few grinds of black pepper. Bring to a simmer.

Add the rice and greens, if using, and cook until tender, about I5 minutes (but maybe longer depending on what grain you use—please reference package directions). Stir in the beans, if using, and simmer until warm. Serve topped with pesto, sauce, crispies, or croutons.

SNACKS
AND A COUPLE OF DRINKS

Left to my own devices, I would eat crackers or chips as—or at least alongside—every meal. Once I tried to give both up for Lent but then couldn't remember what else I ate besides crackers. I hear there are people who can get by on three meals a day. Oh how I would love to go longer than ninety minutes without needing a snack. But I'm the snack captain in this house and my kids are my first mates.

My pantry is rarely without a variety of packaged snacks: Cheez-its, chips, and cheddar bunnies, granola bars, and bags of mixed nuts. But every once in a while I find the snack cabinet bare. Well, not *bare* exactly, but not full of what I *want*. On those occasions I rest easy knowing I can whip up one of the following goodies. The snacks in this chapter are fun and easy to make for casual noshing, but make nice predinner snacks for guests and even work as party favors or hostess gifts. The drinks feel special enough for entertaining, even though they start with regular pantry staples.

One can't live on snacks alone. But with these pantry-friendly recipes in your arsenal, you can try.

SEEDED
CRACKS

Active Time: 10 minutes | Total Time: 40 minutes | Makes about 15

You know those Mary's Gone Crackers crackers? I love those! I wanted to make something that reminded me of them but without having to, like, soak brown rice and dehydrate stuff. Here, the Go-To Pie Dough acts as a base for a variety of seeds. I like a combination of sesame, sunflower, and pumpkin seeds—the ones I have on hand most often. But you can use just one of them—black and white sesame seeds are gorgeous together— or play around with other combos like sunflower and poppy seeds or pumpkin seeds and flax.

1 disk Go-To Pie Dough (page 111)

All-purpose flour, for rolling

1 large egg, lightly beaten

½ teaspoon kosher salt

Freshly ground black pepper

¼ cup mixed seeds such as sesame, sunflower, and/or pumpkin

Pull the dough from the fridge and let it sit on the counter for 15 to 20 minutes. Preheat the oven to 350°F.

Tear off a piece of parchment paper big enough to cover a large baking sheet. Lightly dust the parchment with flour. Roll the pie dough out on the parchment as thin as you can, aiming for the edges of the paper (don't worry about making it round). Transfer the parchment with the dough to a large baking sheet.

Brush the dough with the egg, season with salt and a few grinds of black pepper, and sprinkle with the seeds. Gently roll the rolling pin over the seeds to help them stick. Using a sharp knife or pizza cutter, cut the dough into strips, squares, or diamonds.

Bake until golden brown, about 30 minutes. Let cool completely on the baking sheet before serving or storing. Crackers will keep in an airtight container at room temperature for about a week.

SESAME
CHEDDAR FLATS

Active Time: 15 minutes | Total Time: 45 minutes to 2 hours | Makes 24

I love a big old platter of assorted cheeses and crackers. But I get a little flustered when I show up to a gathering and find a mountain of cheese cubes. It's a chance to partake in forgotten favorites like marbled Colby Jack and dilled Havarti, but how am I supposed to eat those on the butterfly shaped crackers without making a scene? These cheddar crackers combine my loves into one party-appropriate, handheld snack. They're great on their own, but good with more sliced cheese on top.

I cup all-purpose flour

I tablespoon sesame seeds

I tablespoon sugar

I teaspoon kosher salt

½ teaspoon Curry Spice Blend (page 52) or curry powder, optional

I stick cold unsalted butter

I cup grated sharp cheddar or other firm cheese

¼ cup cold water

Whisk together the flour, sesame seeds, sugar, salt, and Curry Spice Blend, if using, in a large bowl. Grate the butter on the large holes of a box grater right over the bowl, tossing with your hands to coat the butter in the flour mixture. Add the cheddar and use your hands to rub the butter and cheese into the flour. Once the mixture feels close to wet sand in texture, add the water and use a fork to stir it into the dough. Turn the dough out onto a lightly floured surface and knead gently to bring it together. Roll the dough into a 2-inch-diameter log, wrap in plastic wrap or parchment paper, and refrigerate until firm, at least 2 hours and up to 3 days (or freeze up to 3 months).

When ready to bake, preheat the oven to 350°F. Using a sharp knife, slice the dough ¼-inch thick and place ½ inch apart on a parchment-lined baking sheet. Bake, rotating the baking sheet halfway through, until golden, 25 to 30 minutes. Let cool. Flats will keep in an airtight container at room temperature about a week.

BIG OLIVE OIL CRACKERS

Active Time: 1 hour | Total Time: 1 hour 30 minutes | Makes 4 big crackers

A friend once made this dough with half the amount of water and oil and it still turned out OK. It's that forgiving. It's fun and squishy, so you can break off a ball or two to hand it over to tiny assistants, too. You can also take it in a number of flavor directions: sprinkle with flaky salt, flaky salt plus pepper, or flavored salt. You can even dust them with cinnamon and sugar (about 1/2 teaspoon and 1 tablespoon respectively per piece of dough) for an extra special treat.

2½ cups all-purpose flour

¾ teaspoon kosher salt

¾ cup cold water

3 tablespoons olive oil, plus more for brushing

1 tablespoon honey or sugar

Flaky salt or one of the flavored salts on page 56, optional

Preheat the oven to 425°F. Whisk together the flour and salt in a large bowl. Make a well in the center and add the water, oil, and honey. Use a wooden spoon to stir until the dough comes together. Turn out onto a lightly floured surface and knead until smooth. Cover with plastic wrap and let rest at room temperature, 30 minutes.

Divide the dough into four pieces. Working with one piece at a time, on a lightly floured surface, roll each piece of dough as thin as you can (the first one will likely be smaller than the last one; the dough will get easier to roll as it rests). Transfer the dough to a baking sheet and brush with a little more oil; season with flaky or flavored salt, if using. Bake until golden and bubbly, 8 to 10 minutes. Let cool slightly on the baking sheet, then transfer to a rack to cool completely. Repeat with remaining dough. Serve whole or break into pieces. Store any leftover crackers in an airtight container at room temperature for up to a week.

CHARRED ONION DIP

Active time: 20 minutes | Total time: 30 minutes | Makes about 1½ cups

I've spent a lot of time caramelizing onions over the years, for dips and other applications, and I'm finally old enough to admit it: that can be really annoying. So much slicing and so much stirring and deglazing and waiting. And, if you ask me, they're a little too sweet in the end. Charring onions under the broiler, on the other hand, is really fast and releases a more complex onion flavor—with a hint of sweetness and a little char. The combo of tangy sour cream or yogurt and mayo keeps this dip appropriate for chips, but you can serve with veggies or crackers if you like.

I large onion (any kind), halved and thinly sliced

2 tablespoons olive oil, divided

I teaspoon kosher salt

Freshly ground black pepper

½ cup mayonnaise

½ cup sour cream or Greek yogurt

½ teaspoon paprika, plus more for serving

½ to I teaspoon white wine vinegar

Chips, preferably potato, for serving

Preheat the broiler with the rack in top position. Toss the onion with the oil, ½ teaspoon salt, and several grinds of black pepper on a rimmed baking sheet. Shake the sheet so the onion settles in an even layer. Broil until beginning to char, about 5 minutes. Toss and continue to broil, tossing one more time, until softened, golden in some spots and charred in others, 5 to 7 minutes more (keep an eye on it—broilers vary greatly in power and presence— you're looking for the onion to be very dark in spots, but they should still be pliable. If they're black and brittle, you've gone too far). Let cool, then chop.

In a small bowl, mix together the mayonnaise, sour cream, paprika, vinegar, the remaining ½ teaspoon salt, and cooked onion. Garnish with a little more paprika and serve with chips.

HERB & SHALLOT YOGURT DIP

Active time: 5 minutes | Total time: 5 minutes | Makes about 1½ cups

I like to entertain, but it can be hard to plan every detail ahead. I'm inevitably scrambling around finding forks or an extra chair, shoving toys in a closet. Despite what I may be lacking in the planning and seating department, I know I can always whip up this dip at the last minute. I serve it with chips, with crackers, or—hmm, what's in the fridge?—carrot and celery sticks. It's zesty, thick, and rich enough so you don't have to eat (or make) a ton of it to satisfy. Which is good because entertaining on the fly often means rifling through the fridge and freezer to see what I can pull together. Cold beer or wine, frozen french fries, and boxed mac 'n' cheese? Let's do this thing! Guests will be so impressed with your dip-whipping skills they'll hardly remember the main course.

I cup plain yogurt, preferably Greek

I medium shallot, finely chopped

Zest and juice of I lemon (about I teaspoon and 2 tablespoons respectively)

I teaspoon kosher salt

Freshly ground black pepper

¼ cup chopped fresh herbs such as parsley, cilantro, mint, basil, dill, and/or chives

Olive oil, for serving

Big Olive Oil Crackers (page 278), chips, and/or crudité for serving

In a medium bowl, combine the yogurt, shallot, zest and lemon juice, salt, a few grinds of black pepper, and the herbs. This dip can be made up to 2 days ahead. When ready to serve, drizzle with olive oil and grind some more black pepper over top. Serve with crackers.

SALT & PEPPER HONEY NUTS

Active time: 15 minutes | Total time: 45 minutes | Makes 2 cups

Right behind crackers and crumb topping, a sweet and salty nut mix is one of my great weaknesses. Use whatever nuts, or a combination, that you have in the freezer, but I'm particularly fond of good old peanuts. Make a double batch (use two baking sheets) around the holidays. Serve them with cocktails, bag up half for gifting, or eat them throughout the season all by yourself.

½ cup honey or maple syrup

1 tablespoon unsalted butter

1½ teaspoons kosher salt

¾ teaspoon freshly ground black pepper

2 cups mixed raw, unsalted nuts

Flaky salt or one of the flavored salts on page 56, optional

Preheat the oven to 350°F. Line a rimmed baking sheet with parchment paper.

Heat the honey, butter, salt, and pepper in a medium pot over medium heat until the butter melts and the foam subsides, about 4 minutes. Add the nuts and stir to coat. Pour the mixture onto the prepared baking sheet and spread into a single layer. Transfer to the oven and bake until the syrup is darkened and bubbling, 8 to 10 minutes.

Carefully stir the nuts to separate. Scatter flaky salt over top. Let cool completely before serving. Store in an airtight container at room temperature for up to 3 weeks.

FRUIT FRESCAS

Active time: 15 minutes | Total time: 15 minutes | Serves about 8

Being pregnant, as I was when writing this recipe, can be fun (Maternity jeans! Body pillows! So much ice cream!). But sometimes it leaves you (just me?) wanting a stiff drink. These refreshing fruity sodas filled the void for me. Aguas frescas are popular throughout Mexico and made with whatever fruits (or vegetables, flowers, even grains) are at their best. They're cooling on hot days, which when you're pregnant are most of them. Make them any time of year with whatever colorful fresh or frozen fruit you have stashed. They feel special like a well-crafted cocktail, but they're easy to make. They're ideal for entertaining drinkers and nondrinkers, too; make them virgin and serve alongside a bottle (or two) of your favorite spirit. As I am no longer pregnant, I assure you they taste great with or without a little tequila.

12 ounces chopped melon, frozen berries, pineapple, or mango

¼ cup fresh lime or lemon juice, plus slices, for serving

2 tablespoons sugar, agave, maple syrup, or honey

Pinch kosher salt

4 cups club soda or seltzer for serving

Process the fruit, lime juice, sugar, and salt in a blender or food processor until smooth. Transfer the fruit puree to a large pitcher (this is a good time to stir in the booze, if using, 2 ounces per person) or divide among glasses. Top with the club soda, give it a little stir, and serve with a slice of lime.

GINGERY CITRUSADE

Active time: 15 minutes | Total time: 30 minutes | Serves 8

Simple syrup is, well, really simple. It's equal parts sugar (lasts forever) and water (currently free), simmered together until the sugar dissolves and the mixture is smooth and pourable. You've probably seen it at coffee shops near the milks and raw sugar packets. It's wonderful for sweetening coffee, tea, or cocktails because it mixes seamlessly with other ingredients and doesn't sink to the bottom of your cup. It's easy to make and you can infuse it with other fragrant ingredients you have in the pantry. Here I use fresh ginger, which I love with citrus, but you could try a handful of fresh mint, thyme, basil, or a sliced fresh chili or a pinch of crushed red pepper flakes for kick.

1 cup sugar

1-inch piece fresh ginger, peeled and thinly sliced

2 cups freshly squeezed lemon, lime, or grapefruit juice (from about 4 large grapefruits, 12 lemons, or 14 limes)

1 to 2 cups vodka, gin, or tequila (optional)

5 to 6 cups club soda or seltzer

Lemon and lime slices, for serving

Combine the sugar, ginger, and 1 cup water in a small pot over medium-high heat. Bring to a boil, stirring occasionally, until the sugar dissolves, about 4 minutes. Set aside to cool.

Strain the ginger syrup and refrigerate until ready to use (the syrup will keep, tightly covered in the refrigerator, for up to a week). When you're ready to serve, place half the syrup in a large pitcher. Add the lemon juice and vodka, if using, stirring well to combine. Taste and add more syrup as desired. Just before serving, add the club soda and serve over ice. Garnish with a slice of lemon.

SWEETS

I still love to bake more than I love to cook. I think it's something about the precise measurements and a false sense of control. For whatever reason—stir-craziness?—snow days and lazy Sundays are when I get the most persistent itch. Sometimes it's too much to bear to suit up for special ingredients. Whether or not it's the weather that keeps you at home, a well-maintained pantry keeps all of these treats well within reach. And you won't even have to leave the house. Itch scratched.

CHOCOLATE
SKILLET CAKE

Active time: 25 minutes | Total time: 55 minutes | Serves 8 to 10

If you don't have an oven-safe skillet, you can make this in a large cake pan. But baking directly in a skillet helps the cake stay warm longer (better for ice cream meltage) and makes for easier reheating. Although, I guess you could zap a piece in the microwave for fifteen seconds to a similar end. Whatever you bake it in, I suggest scooping the cake versus slicing. The messier it lands in the bowl, the better, since cracks and crevices offer more opportunities for the ice cream to soak in.

I stick (½ cup) unsalted butter, cut into pieces, plus more for skillet

8 ounces semi- or bittersweet chocolate chips or chopped chocolate

¾ cup sugar, divided

I teaspoon pure vanilla extract

¾ teaspoon kosher salt

4 large eggs, separated, at room temperature

¼ cup all-purpose flour

Ice cream, any flavor, for serving

Caramel Sauce (page 86), for serving, optional

Preheat the oven to 350°F. Butter a 10-inch ovenproof skillet and set aside.

Melt the chocolate and the I stick butter in a large microwave-safe bowl, stirring every 30 seconds until smooth and combined (alternately, you can melt the chocolate and butter in a large heat-safe bowl set over a medium pot filled with an inch of simmering water). Let cool slightly.

Whisk ½ cup sugar into the chocolate mixture until evenly combined. Whisk in the vanilla, salt, and egg yolks. Scatter the flour over top and whisk to combine.

Using an electric mixer on medium-high speed, beat the egg whites until foamy, about I minute. Add the remaining ¼ cup sugar and beat until the whites are glossy and hold soft peaks—this can happen fast, so don't walk away with the mixer running. When you lift up a beater the whites should gracefully bow like a ballerina. Fold about a third of the egg whites into the chocolate mixture until the batter is streaky. Repeat with another third of the whites. Fold the remaining third of the whites into the chocolate mixture until *just* combined (too much mixing and you'll deflate those voluminous whites). Transfer to the prepared skillet and bake until the top looks dry and cracked, 30 to 35 minutes. Serve warm with ice cream, drizzled with caramel, if using.

FOOD PROCESSOR
RAINBOW SORBET

Active time: 25 minutes | Total time: 2 hours 25 minutes | Serves 8 to 10

Rainbow sherbet from Baskin-Robbins—or "31 Flavors" as we used to call it—was my standard ice cream order as a kid. I can still taste the tropical trio: the icy, tongue-tingling combination of pineapple, orange, and raspberry. I am a firm believer that just because you can make something at home doesn't necessarily mean you should. But there was something so deeply satisfying about approximating a childhood favorite with my own two hands and a couple of bags of frozen fruit that I couldn't resist. Plus, it's a great way to use up any frozen fruit if you're tired of smoothies or cake (does this happen?). You don't have to make this recipe in its entirety. Make one flavor of sorbet (with whatever frozen fruit you have) and call it a day.

I pint pineapple or coconut sorbet or vanilla ice cream

8 to 10 ounces frozen mango or peaches

I banana, peeled and sliced, or I cup frozen peaches

½ cup sugar, divided

Kosher salt

8 to 10 ounces frozen raspberries, strawberries, or blackberries

> Another good riff to try: strawberry sorbet with store-bought chocolate and vanilla ice cream for an updated Neapolitan.

Remove the sorbet from the freezer and set it on the counter to soften slightly. Line an 8- or 9-inch baking dish with plastic wrap, leaving a generous overhang on the sides.

Combine the mango, half of the banana, ¼ cup sugar, and a pinch of salt in a food processor and pulse until coarsely chopped. Continue to process, scraping down the sides of the bowl if necessary, until smooth, about 3 minutes. Scrape mango mixture into the prepared baking dish. Don't worry about smoothing it out yet.

Repeat with the raspberries, the remaining banana and ¼ cup sugar, and another pinch of salt (no need to wash the machine in between) and transfer the mixture to the baking dish.

Dump the sorbet into the baking dish and, using a spatula, gently swirl the three flavors together. Cover with the plastic wrap and freeze until firm, at least 2 hours and up to 2 weeks.

MY BEST
BANANA BREAD

Active time: 10 minutes | Total time: 1 hour 10 minutes, plus cooling | Makes 1 loaf

Banana bread recipes are like opinions: everybody's got one. Many years ago I was assigned the task of developing a recipe for the BEST banana bread. Every person I worked with offered their favorite version—I think there were nine in total. In almost every case, it was the banana bread their mom or dad or Aunt Joan made, the one they ate growing up. They ranged from pale and dry to decadent and chocolate studded; dense and squat to lofty and cakelike. Some of these quick breads, while dearly beloved, just weren't very good. (Pro tip: never trust a banana bread recipe that calls for fewer than three bananas.) And even after we collectively agreed on a single recipe as our B.E.S.T. best, everyone quietly admitted they still preferred their original submission.

Nostalgia is a powerful thing. It's an impossible task to try and create the "best" of anything because everything (except math), most certainly food, is subjective. This banana bread is my best, and it's one of the best I've ever had. It's almost identical to the one I grew up eating, adapted from a cookbook called Recipes for Healthier Children: A Mother's Guide, *by Edith Redman (1973). It's deeply browned yet still tender, thanks to the bananas and brown sugar. I added yogurt for more body, toasted walnuts for crunch (you could use pecans), and streusel because I couldn't resist. It is squishy and moist and best eaten spread with softened cream cheese. Because that's how we ate it growing up. There's a good chance you'll like this one better than your mom's (I promise I won't tell).*

¼ cup (½ stick) unsalted butter, melted, plus more for baking pan

1½ cups all-purpose flour

1 teaspoon baking soda

¾ teaspoon kosher salt

3 large (or 4 small to medium) very ripe bananas, mashed (about 1½ cups)

1 cup (packed) dark brown sugar

¼ cup whole-milk Greek yogurt, or sour cream

2 large eggs

1 teaspoon pure vanilla extract

½ cup chopped toasted walnuts or pecans (optional)

½ cup All-Purpose Streusel (page 119), optional

Preheat the oven to 350°F with a rack in the middle position. Coat a standard 8½-by-4½-inch loaf pan with a little butter and line with parchment paper and set aside. Whisk together the flour, baking soda, and salt in a large bowl.

In a separate bowl, combine the bananas with the brown sugar, yogurt, ¼ cup butter, eggs, and vanilla until evenly combined. Add the wet ingredients to the dry and stir until just combined. Fold in the walnuts, if using.

Transfer the mixture to the prepared pan and top with the streusel, if using. Bake until very dark brown and a toothpick inserted in the center comes out clean, just about 1 hour. Let cool before slicing. Banana bread will keep, tightly wrapped at room temperature, up to 4 days.

UNIVERSAL YOGURT CAKE

Active time: 10 minutes | **Total time: 1 to 2 hours** | **Makes one 9-inch cake**

What I love about this cake—besides how moist and tender it is, how well it freezes, and the crunchy sugar topping—is that you can bake it in whatever baking pan you have. Round or square? Yep. Loaf pan? Done that (70 to 75 minutes). I even see your muffin tin wanting a piece of the action (20 to 25 minutes). Make it with whatever frozen or fresh fruit you have on hand. Also, I've made this recipe with milk or buttermilk in place of the yogurt, and it even works with nondairy options like almond milk or oat milk. It's endlessly adaptable and always delicious.

½ cup vegetable oil, plus more for pan

½ cup plain whole-milk yogurt

3 large eggs

1 tablespoon pure vanilla extract

1 cup plus 2 tablespoons sugar, divided

2 teaspoons baking powder

¾ teaspoon kosher salt

1½ cups plus 1 tablespoon all-purpose flour, divided

2 cups frozen berries

Preheat the oven to 350°F. Brush a 9-inch-square baking pan with oil and line the bottom with parchment paper. Set aside. Whisk together the oil, yogurt, eggs, vanilla, and 1 cup sugar in a medium bowl. In a separate bowl, whisk together the baking powder, salt, and 1½ cups flour to combine. Whisk the wet ingredients into the dry until just combined. Toss the berries with the remaining 1 tablespoon flour. Fold into the batter and transfer to the prepared pan.

Sprinkle evenly with the remaining 2 tablespoons sugar. Bake until golden and a toothpick inserted in the middle comes out clean, 50 to 55 minutes. Let cool slightly before serving. Cake will keep, tightly wrapped at room temperature, up to 4 days. But it freezes really well; wrap tightly and freeze for up to 3 months.

BROWN BUTTER CHOCOLATE CHIP COOKIES

Active time: 15 minutes | Total time: 45 minutes | Makes about 24

I've never loved chocolate. When I was little, my mom would always bake some of the chocolate chip cookie dough without chocolate chips just for me. (What a mom!) Even now, I like chocolate, but I'll always pick a fruit dessert first. What I wanted to do with this recipe was make the dough part as good as the chocolate part so they taste as special to the chocolate likers as they do to the lovers. If you don't have chocolate bars you can use chocolate chips or chopped chocolate if that's what you prefer. But the puddles of chocolate that big pieces create are pretty special, even for someone like me.

1 cup (2 sticks) unsalted butter, at room temperature

½ cup packed brown sugar (light or dark is OK)

½ cup granulated sugar

2 teaspoons pure vanilla extract

1 large egg

1¾ cups all-purpose flour

1 teaspoon kosher salt

½ teaspoon baking soda

8 ounces milk or semisweet chocolate, preferably bars, broken up into 1-inch pieces

1 cup chopped toasted pecans, walnuts, or hazelnuts, optional

Preheat the oven to 375°F . Line two baking sheets with parchment paper. Set aside.

Melt 1 stick butter in a small skillet or saucepan over medium heat, swirling occasionally, until brown and nutty smelling, about 4 minutes. Let cool to room temperature.

Using an electric mixer, beat the remaining 1 stick of butter with the brown and granulated sugars on medium high until creamy, about 3 minutes. Stream in the brown butter and beat to combine. Stop the mixer and scrape down the sides of the bowl to make sure everything is combined. Add vanilla and the egg and beat to combine. Stop the mixer and scrape down the sides of the bowl again.

Whisk the flour, salt, and baking soda in a medium bowl. With the mixer on low, gradually add the flour mixture and beat to combine. Dump in the chocolate and beat on low until evenly incorporated. Fold in the nuts, if using.

Scoop balls (about 2 tablespoons per cookie) of dough onto the prepared baking sheets and bake, rotating halfway through, until the cookies are golden brown on the bottom, 10 to 12 minutes. Let cool as long as you can wait.

HALF-BAKED
PEANUT BUTTER PIE

Active time: 40 minutes | Total time: 1 hour, 25 minutes | Serves 8

Because it has a couple of moving parts, this pie looks more complicated to make than it actually is. Bottom line: if you can make whipped cream you can nail this pie. The salty cracker crust against the creamy peanut butter filling is a knockout combination. Topped with whipped cream and cocktail peanuts, it might make you swoon it's so good. Be warned: the peanut butter mousse filling is delicious on its own.

CRUST
6 ounces Ritz crackers, saltines, graham crackers, or chocolate wafer cookies (about 1½ sleeves Ritz, saltines, or grahams)

1 tablespoon sugar

Pinch kosher salt

6 tablespoons unsalted butter, melted

FILLING
1 cup Greek yogurt (preferably full fat)

1 cup peanut butter, or other nut butter (smooth or crunchy)

¼ teaspoon kosher salt

½ cup light or dark brown sugar, divided

2 cups heavy cream, divided

¼ cup roasted salted peanuts, crushed

MAKE THE CRUST
Preheat the oven to 350°F. Combine the crackers, sugar, and salt in a food processor and process until finely ground (you should get about 1½ cups). If you don't have a food processor, place in a resealable plastic bag and bang and roll with a rolling pin or meat mallet until crushed. Add the melted butter and pulse until the mixture looks like wet sand.

Dump the cracker mixture into a standard 9-inch pie plate. Using the bottom of a flat-bottom measuring cup or water glass, press the mixture into the bottom and up the sides of the pie plate. Bake on the middle rack until dry and golden brown, 20 to 25 minutes. Let cool.

MAKE THE FILLING
Whisk the yogurt, peanut butter, salt, and ¼ cup brown sugar in a large bowl. In a separate bowl, using an electric mixer, beat 1 cup of cream and the remaining ¼ cup brown sugar until stiff peaks form. Working in three additions, fold the whipped cream into the peanut butter mixture until evenly incorporated; transfer to the cooled crust and smooth the top. Freeze until just firm, at least 3 hours and up to 2 days. (Once set in the freezer, you can transfer the pie to the refrigerator where it will remain firm yet sliceable for a couple of days.)

HALF-BAKED
PEANUT BUTTER PIE

If pulling straight from the freezer, let the pie sit at room temperature about 30 minutes before serving (this will make it easier to slice). When ready to serve, whip the remaining I cup cream to soft peaks; pile on top of the pie and top with crushed peanuts.

Flip the script: Make the peanut butter filling and chill in bowls or glasses in the fridge. Top with whipped cream, crushed crackers, and peanuts.

ALMOND CORNMEAL CRUMB BARS

Active time: 35 minutes | Total time: 2 hours, 35 minutes | Makes about 12

When you work in restaurants, all the cooks have a notebook. In it you are to record recipes and/or vague associated wisdom so you can refer to them throughout the day's dinner preparation. Every professional cook I know preserved their notebooks, referencing golden ratios for everything from yeasted rolls to baba au rhum. I don't think I was a complete dum-dum (though I was a young twenty-three), but I totally missed the boat on this one. I tossed my notebooks one of the times I moved between that first restaurant job and now (there have been nine "permanent addresses"). It pains me to think of what was lost to paper recycling: recipes for cakes and caramels and candied peel, perfect custards and pot de crème. I've tried to re-create some of them, but they're never quite the same as I remember.

Like this recipe, which is based on a fregolotta, *a shortbread-type cookie often served with ice cream at Chez Panisse in Berkeley, California, where my boss had been a pastry cook. It is one of my all-time favorite cookies, because it is essentially* all *crumb topping. I never could locate the original recipe so I've made it into a bar, added a layer of fruit and experimented with different nuts. While it may not be the same as the original (who could say?) I like this version a lot. As usual, it's adaptable: use the nuts and berries that you prefer.*

I cup (2 sticks) unsalted butter, at room temperature, plus more for baking dish

¾ cup raw almonds, pecans, or hazelnuts, or I cup almond or other nut meal

2 cups all-purpose flour

½ cup yellow cornmeal

¾ teaspoon kosher salt, plus a pinch

I cup sugar, divided

I teaspoon pure vanilla extract

3 cups fresh or frozen berries

I tablespoon lemon juice

Preheat the oven to 350°F. Butter an 8- or 9-inch square baking dish and line with parchment paper, leaving a I-inch overhang on two sides. Set aside. In a food processor, pulse the almonds until finely ground (you should have about I cup). In a large bowl, whisk together the ground nuts, flour, cornmeal, and ¾ teaspoon salt. Set aside.

In a medium bowl, combine the I cup butter and ¾ cup sugar and mix with an electric mixer on medium high until creamy, about 3 minutes. Add the vanilla and beat to combine. With the mixer on low, add the flour mixture and beat until crumbly. Press about two-thirds of the dough into the prepared dish.

In a medium bowl, toss the berries with the lemon juice, the remaining ¼ cup sugar, and a pinch of salt; scatter the mixture over the bottom crust and crumble the remaining dough over top, squeezing it together to make big chunks. Bake until golden brown, 55 to 60 minutes. Let cool in the dish on a wire rack before cutting into squares or bars.

SPARKLY JAM & NUT TART

Active time: 10 minutes | Total time: 1 hour | Serves 8

Here's another one of my favorite riffable emergency desserts. I often throw it together if I'm entertaining unexpectedly because it's super easy (if I have pie dough in the freezer) and really pretty. You know the drill by now: use any nut you like and your favorite jam. Some combinations I'm awfully fond of are apricot jam and pistachios (pictured), raspberry jam and peanuts, or blackberry or cherry and hazelnuts. Be sure to bake your tart on a rack set in the lower third position of the oven. This helps the bottom of the tart get nice and golden at the same rate as the top. Baking to a deep golden brown also ensures the leftovers are sturdy and portable.

¼ cup toasted nuts

2 tablespoons sugar

Pinch kosher salt

1 round Go-To Pie Dough
(page 111)

¾ cup store-bought jam or Frozen
Fruit Jam (page 86)

1 egg, beaten

Preheat the oven to 350°F with the rack in lower third position. Place the nuts, sugar, and salt in a food processor and process until the nuts are mostly sandy (some bigger bits are OK). Alternately, place everything in a plastic bag and bang with a rolling pin.

On a lightly floured surface, roll the pie dough to a 15-inch circle (you're going for ⅛-inch thickness; it really doesn't matter what shape it is). Spread the jam over the dough, leaving a 2-inch border. Fold the dough over the jam and brush the edges with the egg. Sprinkle with the nut and sugar mixture. Bake until golden brown, 40 to 45 minutes. Let cool before slicing.

TOASTED
OAT BISCUITS

Active time: 20 minutes | Total Time: 3 hours | Makes about 30 cookies

These cookies are based on a recipe I first developed in 2009 for Valentine's Day. Those cookies required chilling and rolling and cutting into hearts, then sandwiching with Nutella. Not bad, but more work than I'm interested in the other 364 days of the year. To simplify things, I roll the dough into logs and refrigerate it for slicing and baking. Interesting discovery, though: while you can slice and bake these as soon as 2 hours after you make the dough, they're definitely more tender if they sit in the fridge a bit longer, up to 5 days. Reason enough to keep a log on hand, just in case.

I cup old-fashioned rolled oats, divided

2 cups all-purpose flour

¾ teaspoon kosher salt

I cup (2 sticks) unsalted butter, room temperature

¾ cup packed light or dark brown sugar

I teaspoon pure vanilla extract

I large egg, lightly beaten

Place the oats in a large skillet over medium heat. Cook, stirring often, until slightly dark and nutty smelling, about 5 minutes. Let cool. Reserve ¼ cup of oats. Transfer the remaining ¾ cup oats to a medium bowl; stir in the flour and salt.

In a large bowl, using an electric mixer, beat the butter and brown sugar on medium until fluffy, about 3 minutes. Add the vanilla and beat to combine. Scrape down the bowl. Add ¾ cup of oat mixture and beat to combine. Divide the dough in half and form into two logs, each about 2 inches in diameter. Wrap in plastic and refrigerate until firm, at least 2 hours or up to 5 days. Dough can be frozen for up to 3 months.

Preheat the oven to 350°F, with racks in upper and lower thirds. Line 2 baking sheets with parchment paper. Set aside. Slice the logs into ¼-inch-thick rounds and place on the prepared baking sheets. Brush with the egg and sprinkle with the reserved ¼ cup oats. Bake, rotating the sheets halfway through, until the cookies are golden around the edges, 12 to 14 minutes. Let cool completely on the sheet. Store in an airtight container at room temperature for about a week.

MAGIC HONEY SESAME STICKS

Active time: 30 minutes | Total time: 30 minutes | Makes about 24 sticks

Typically, I avoid deep-frying at home—it can be kind of scary dealing with that much hot oil and, depending on what's fried, potentially smelly. But these strips of fried pie dough are so worth it. Cut the dough into squares or diamonds, or punch out shapes with cookie cutters. They're excellent eaten slightly warm, but you can store any leftovers in an airtight container at room temperature for about 5 days, where they stay slightly crisp even after prolonged soaking in honey. I don't understand how this happens. Probably magic.

1 round Go-To Pie Dough
(page 111)

¾ cup honey

2 strips orange zest, optional

Vegetable oil, for frying

All-purpose flour, for rolling

2 tablespoons toasted sesame seeds

Flaky salt, optional

If using premade pie dough, remove from the fridge and let it sit on the counter for about 20 minutes.

Combine the honey and orange zest, if using, in a small pot or skillet and set over low heat.

Fill a heavy-bottomed pot with about 2 inches of oil (for a medium pot, this will take 4 to 6 cups of oil). Heat over medium heat and fit with a deep-fry/candy thermometer if you have one. If you have a thermometer, you're looking for 350°F.

On a lightly floured surface, roll the dough to about ⅛-inch thick. Cut into squares, diamonds, or strips. (You can even tie strips into pretzel shapes or ribbon shapes, pressing gently so they hold together.)

Drop one piece of dough into the hot oil; it should sizzle vigorously but not in a scary way. Add as many pieces of dough as will fit comfortably and fry, turning halfway through, until golden brown, about 5 minutes. Using tongs or a slotted spoon, transfer each cookie to the honey mixture and turn to coat. Transfer to a plate and sprinkle with the sesame seeds and a little salt, if using.

WHIPPED CREAM

Active time: 5 minutes | Total time: 5 minutes | Serves 6

Every year for my sister's birthday, my mom would make her a cake drowning in homemade whipped cream. It was a split and hollowed-out angel-food cake, inside of which she spooned a mixture of canned chopped pineapple, strawberries, mini marshmallows, and whipped cream. The ambrosia-like mixture was sandwiched between the layers of tender cake and covered with more whipped cream.

We were a canned whipped cream house, but the homemade version is so easy to make that I'm not sure why it was reserved for this one birthday alone. These days, my family insists I make homemade whipped cream whenever the opportunity presents itself—birthdays, holidays, Thursdays. Once you're reminded how superior to the canned stuff it tastes, you'll be creating all sorts of opportunities to make it yourself.

This recipe makes about 3 cups of whipped cream—enough to put out on the dessert buffet at holiday time—but if you need less just do the division and proceed. Use it on pie, fresh berries, or instead of regular frosting on your next birthday cake. One of my favorite ways to use it is in place of (or in addition to) ice cream in a sundae-like preparation. Layer it with chocolate or caramel sauce or a few spoonfuls of jam and crumbled cookies, crackers, or nuts.

2 cups heavy cream

2 tablespoons powdered sugar, granulated sugar, maple syrup, or honey

½ teaspoon pure vanilla extract

In the bowl of an electrix mixer, comine the cream, powdered sugar, and vanilla and whip on medium speed until soft peaks form, about 4 minutes (watch carefully, since all mixers and pints of cream are not created equal). Whipped cream can be made up to 2 hours ahead. Refrigerate until ready to use. Stir gently with a spatula before serving.

READY, SET, EAT

Page numbers in italics refer to images.